MORE RAG RUGS

& Recycled Textile Projects

CRAFTWORLD SERIES

ACKNOWLEDGEMENTS

I would like to thank:

Molly Walker for her proof reading and sense of humour; Lorenzo for his illustrations and patience; all the makers who have contributed their work and those who shared memories. For letting me photograph their vintage rugs: Beamish Museum, Berrington Hall, the Museum in the Park, Nantwich Museum, Pontypool Museum and the Thomas Shop. Also the anonymous enthusiasts in Rug Yarns and anyone I have left out (you know who you are) and my best friend Finn.

TRAPLET
PUBLICATIONS

Published in 2011
by Traplet Publications Limited,
Traplet House, Pendragon Close, Malvern,
Worcestershire WR14 1GA

Text © Jenni Stuart-Anderson
The Birches, Middleton-on-the-Hill, Leominster,
Herefordshire HR6 0HN

Photographs © Jenni Stuart-Anderson, or:
page 4, 115 Keith James; page 35 June Emmerson,
Eileen Scholes; page 66 Yvonne Autie; page 69, 70 Caroline
Marriott; page 88 Zia Rahim; pages 93, 95, 104, 108 Steve
Heavens; page 101 Richard Stanton©.
Photographs on the Gallery pages supplied by the artists.

Illustrations by Lorenzo Gavarini
© Jenni Stuart-Anderson

ISBN 978-1-907712-07-4
British Library Cataloguing in Publication Data
A catalogue recording for this book is available from the British Library

Designed by Julie Arnett
Set in Myriad and Rockwell

Printed by Warners, Bourne, Lincolnshire

MORE RAG RUGS

& Recycled Textile Projects

Jenni Stuart-Anderson

My grandad used to make rag rugs when I was a little girl, sitting by the black iron stove on winter evenings listening to the radio. It's an image as clear as day even now and for me was about warmth and family and security. I never learnt then, and by the time I was old enough to be really interested in making them, he had passed on to readicut rugs which didn't interest me at all. Part of the joy for me now is making something out of something that has been discarded. Recently my mother gave me the little antler my grandad used to prod with – which was a fabulous gift.
Anon

INTRODUCTION

Rag rug making is a hands-on 'grandmother skill', passed from one generation to another. It resurfaces in times of austerity when people need to 'make do and mend' again. As I write, recycling and sewing are all the rage and making and mending techniques, which had almost died out, are the subject of popular courses. All over the country 'stitch and bitch' and 'knit and natter' groups have sprung up where people of different ages share skills such as knitting and crochet.

Here are some exciting new projects to make from recycled textiles, using traditional rag rug methods, plus a pegloomed project. Basics like History, Colour and Design are included with some things I have learned since I wrote my first book. I have invited some creative women to share their unique projects for you to make. I hope you will be inspired to have a go and that one project leads to another, and you enjoy it as much as I do.

Also in this book you will find more quotations by people who have seen me demonstrating and have shared their memories about the times when most poor people made mats from their old clothes because that was all they could afford to provide a bit of comfort in their cold homes.

> " My great grandmother had a frame and used half a peg.
> Everyone who visited had to peg enough to cover their feet. "
> Yorks.

Making rag rugs should be a cheap, creative way of re-using worn clothes and furnishings – it has always been about improvising so take the instructions as a starting point. It is easier if you use the right tool for the technique but in the early days they improvised the tools too.

> " We wrapped rags around a 6 inch nail and pushed them
> through. We had to use old sacks 'cause we couldn't afford
> hessian. My dad said: 'Come on, let's do an hour on the rug' "

For me, it all started when I was at home with my baby daughter in 1985 and felt the need for a creative hobby which I could fit around childcare - something that didn't cost much. I remembered seeing some lovely rag rugs in a friend's house and asked him for the maker's details. Mrs Doris Tunley was pleased by my interest in the rugs she had been making since her childhood, when she had spent time in bed, recuperating from an operation. Her mum had said, "Here's a sack and half a clothes peg. Cut up these old clothes and make a proddy mat." She kept making them for more than 50 years and since she showed me how to do it, I haven't stopped, either!

When Doris's husband Stan died she said, referring to herself: "If it 'ent your turn, you canna go". Finally, in 2010, it was her turn so, sadly, she will not see this book.

Making rag rugs gives me a sense of connection with the people who have treasured and re-used textiles through the generations. I am grateful to Mrs Tunley for sharing her skills, which I now pass on to you.

CONTENTS

Vintage proddy mat at Farfield Mill, Cumbria

Vintage hooked mat at the Thomas Shop

Mat hooked by Laura May Baker (born 1875), Northumberland. 136 x 104cm (53½ x 41in). Beamish Museum

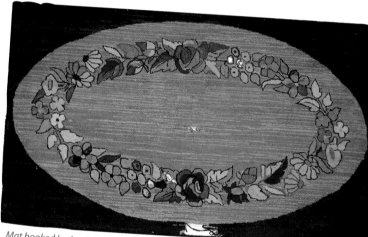

Mat hooked by Annie Margaret Roddam in Northumberland in the early 1900s. 129 x 74cm (51 x 29in). Beamish Museum

Hooked mat circa 1916, Northumberland. 157 x 73.5cm (62 x 29in). Beamish Museum

Vintage hooked mat from Louisiana, 200 x 140cm (78 x 55in). Collection of the author

CONNECTING THREADS
historical perspective

Spinning and weaving have been done by women since early times because both activities are compatible with child watching. They were repetitive tasks, which could be stopped and started as required and were safe around children. As breast feeding would have continued for years, women's productive labour was home based. Remains of what appear to have been simple looms, located where the light from the entrance fell, and adjacent to the hearth, have been excavated in Hungary in Neolithic huts from around 5500 B.C.E.

Women spun thread whilst doing other things and in some countries, like Peru, can still be seen spinning with drop spindles, whilst travelling. Many hours were spent on the gathering and preparation of flax to weave linen and in the temperate zone, where clothing was required all year round, girls spun as they watched over sheep. Then there was shearing, cleaning fleece, carding, more spinning, and later dyeing and weaving the wool, so production of textiles was a major part of women's lives.

Women weaving on a Grecian warp-weighted loom. Drawing from Athenian vase painting about 560 B.C.E.

Spinning and weaving goddesses abound in the mythology of ancient cultures all over the world. However, in Navajo creation stories there were also male weavers. Weaving woollen yarn on large looms was heavy work which, by the middle ages, was done mainly by men.

In 1337, a Proclamation of Edward III offered "the King's protection and safe conduct" to "…cloth workers of strange lands, of whatsoever country they be…", encouraging them to settle in England to help develop the industry. After Henry VIII broke off relations with the Catholic Church in 1534, England received many Protestants escaping persecution throughout Europe, including Flemish weavers, who were skilled at their craft and introduced many innovations.

In the eighteenth century cloth was used for bedding and clothing. Because of the considerable time and energy involved in its production it was patched and mended until eventually it was used for rag weaving of bedspreads, and later for rugs, in Sweden and Canada. 'Couvertures de marriage' were woven in strips by French Acadians of the Canadian Maritime Provinces. When the British conquered Acadia, renaming it Nova Scotia around 1713, many Acadians fled to Louisiana where their culture still survives.

In Northern Japan peasants began weaving cotton rags into strips on backstrap looms in the 1750s. These saki-ori were sewn into heavy kimono style housecoats (yogi), worn in the day and used at night as bedding. The woven strips were also sewn together as kotatsugake, heavy coverlets that were placed over small traditional heaters around which a family would sit, warming their hands and feet under the coverlet. Kotatsugakes were sometimes also used as floor rugs.

Imported cotton became very popular in Britain in the 18th century, much of it from America where it was grown with slave labour:

> " *But now cotton yarn is cheaper than linen yarn and cotton goods are very much used in place of cambrics, lawns and other expensive fabrics of flax; they have almost superceded the silks. Women of all ranks, from the highest to the lowest, are clothed in British manufactures of cotton.* "
> MacPhersons's Annals of Commerce 1785.

Early coverings for floors of earth, stone or wood had been straw or rushes, and sand was spread on kitchen floors to be swept up when dirty. Handmade textiles, too precious to be used on floors, were displayed on tables and chests. Until about 1820 bed 'ruggs' were made by sewing yarn loops on linen backing.

Worn-out clothing and linen were made into plaited (braided) rugs and patchwork quilts and sewn, poked or hooked into a woven linen base to make rugs. In the 1850s jute hessian (burlap) from India became commercially available in Europe and in North America where rug hooking became widely practised, developing into a rich folk art, continued to the present.

In nineteenth century North America rags were collected, cut, and sewn into strips, then wound into balls at home and sent away to be woven by full-time weavers:

> " *If you double twist the warp yourself the weaver will charge 6d (six pence) a yard for the weaving, but if he doubles and twists he charges 8d.* "
> Peter Lund Smith writing about Canada in 1862
> (Waste Products and Underdeveloped Substances)

In England cloth had been produced in the Stroud Valleys in Gloucestershire since medieval times, and was exported in such quantities that, at one time, 170 mills were in simultaneous production. So famous were the Stroud Valleys for their woollen broadcloth that the word 'stroud' became a general term for broadcloth (high quality plain woven cloth with smooth felted appearance). Dyed red, blue, green or black, it was traded in the 18th century from Nova Scotia to Louisiana, recognised by the undyed selvedges, known as 'lists' or 'worms'. British soldiers were known as 'Redcoats' from the late 17th century and stroud broadcloth was even used in Native American artifacts. Cloth from the Gigg Mill was bought by the East India Company to sell in India and China.

> " *As we approach Nailsworth the mills become more frequent. Tall chimneys rise up from the low lands and their black tops send forth forbidding streams of thick smoke. About a mile from the village, a huge cloth mill (Dunkirk), factory-like, gloomy, many-windowed, and populous with young persons and adults, all with their arms and hands more or less dyed the colour of black cloth, and all more or less busy in their respective departments of labour. ...The only sound by which you may at once recognise the vicinity of cloth mills is a heavy, dull beating, a ponderous thump-bump-thump-bump, which awakens you in the morning and keeps you awake at night...*
>
> *On Sunday mornings every beater in every mill is quiet... the great water-wheels... are now motionless, the whole valley is free from the clouds of rolling smoke. The sluggish river, too, has its day of rest, and runs lazily, securely by, no longer entrapped in mill dams and seduced*

COMBING WHEEL.

Combing wheel

into side channels. The large bleaching and drying grounds show their empty framework of wood unclothed and bare; nor does scarlet cloth today flaunt its glaring brightness in the sun….for once in the week you may listen to birds singing in the thickets, and behold streams running unpolluted with madder or any other kind of dye.
The Minister of Lower Shortwood Chapel 1865 "

The industrial revolution, which started in England in the 18th century, led to profound changes throughout society, spreading to Europe and America. Weaving kept pace with improved spinning technology by employing more (male) handloom weavers. The availability of cheap Irish labour delayed the mechanisation of weaving, but eventually manufacturers found that it was cheaper to employ women and children to work power looms. 'Parish' or 'pauper apprentices', as young as seven, were relocated from cities to mills where they worked 16 hour days for basic food and lodging until they reached the age of 21, if they survived. Many such children were bought from workhouses and orphanages by mill owners, for a pittance.

"They took me into the counting house and showed me a piece of paper with a red sealed horse on which they told me to touch, and then to make a cross, which I did. This meant I had to stay at Cressbrook Mill till I was twenty one." Sarah Carpenter, interviewed in The Ashton Chronicle (23rd June, 1849) "

Child apprentices in textile factory. Apprentice greeting former friend, the workers in rags. From :' Life and adventures of Michael Armstrong, the factory boy' by Frances Trollope, 1876. Wellcome Library, London

A view of Leeds from 'The Graphic' of 1885 which shows mills and workers' houses

The harsh economic climate and difficult working conditions in the new textile factories generated a movement in 1811 of hand weavers opposed to the new automated looms that could be operated by cheap, unskilled labour, resulting in the loss of many jobs. They were called the Luddites, after militant weaver, Ned Ludd. The unrest spread from Nottingham to other areas: mills and machinery were burned by handloom weavers who clashed with the army, leading to their trial, executions and penal transportations.

At the start of the nineteenth century there were only three mills in Bradford, Yorkshire, rising to more than a hundred as it became the centre for worsted manufacture. The population of Bradford in 1831 was 26,309 and by 1851 rose to 103,782 as a result of the great market for the trade.

"My mother was a weaver in a mill and used old clothes to make rugs. We kids cut diamonds called lists. The frame circulated, so every so often it came to us. You paid the owner 2/6d."
(two shillings and six pence) nr. Leeds "

Jaquard weaving shed – from The Young Woman's Companion (1800's)

Drawing in worsted*

Drawing in slivers*

*from The Young Woman's Companion (1800's)

Rag rug commemorating the Jubilee of Queen Victoria in 1887. Beamish Museum

Making rag rugs at home became commonplace from the 1880s, either from old clothes or from mill waste and, in the homes of the rich they were produced by the servants, 'below stairs'. In the UK the most common type was the proddy mat usually made by whole families with the children often allowed only to cut the pieces, graduating later to prodding them.

Rug patterns, first stencilled, later printed on hessian (burlap) were produced commercially in North America in the mid 19th century, and in England from about 1900.

Prodded rag rug in the Edwardian butler's pantry (1901-1910) at Berrington Hall, Herefordshire

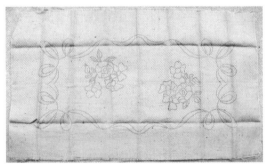

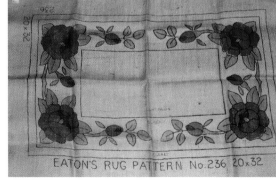

Early stamped commercial rug patterns

EATON'S RUG PATTERN No.236 20x32

Proddy rug on a Barlow stamped hessian. Wool rags, 202 x 122cm (about 79 x 48in). Beamish Museum

Hooky mat, probably made on stamped hessian. 186 x 110cm (77 x 43in)
Wool rags**.

" My mother was from near Durham and I was born there, then we moved to Hartlepool where I live now. I'm 83 (2002). They used to chew toffees when they were making rag rugs to keep the fluff from going on their lungs. It's like the miners – my father used to chew tobacco down the mine and spit it out. It kept the dust from their lungs. The men couldn't afford it buf they were given it, if they'd work an extra shift. "

Group of miners, second from the left is John William Bell (b1882 at Hendon, Sunderland). He developed a trade of making mat hooks which he sold throughout the North East, marked RY Bell. He was a Ryhope blacksmith and sold thousands through the Co-op and other stores.

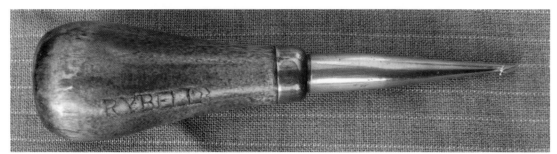

Rug Hook marked RYBell

Unusual hooked mat from Hexham area of Northumberland, probably late 1800s. Woollen rags, 156 x 86cms (61 x 38in). Beamish Museum

The Novelty Rug Machine was invented in the 1880s in Ohio and sold by the American Rug Pattern Company in Maine. Various patented rug making tools became available and were used enthusiastically by those fortunate enough to afford them in America and Britain. They were sold by wool companies for wool rugs but some people substituted the expensive rug wool with strips of rag. One such tool was the Latchet Hook which was designed to loop and knot the wool: many people have asked me if I knot the rags, as they remember their elders doing, years ago.

Rug Making

A Pleasant Useful and Profitable Indoor Occupation

William Jones &Co
RUG-WOOL MERCHANTS
Bridgnorth

22in. wide Rug, Design No. 5

Your Foot does the Work

The "Airlyne" Rugmaker attached to a Dining Table

The "Airlyne" Rugmaker is a foot-operated machine incorporating a special streamlined needle which *glides* through the canvas. A speed of 100 loops per minute is easily attained.

With very little practice exceptionally even stitches are produced, which, of course, saves wool, and in a short time the most complicated designs are easily accomplished in a fraction of the time previously required using a hand needle.

The "Airlyne" Rugmaker is quickly fitted to any table by means of adjustable clamps. The rug backing is placed on the table and drawn over the platform. On depressing the foot the needle thrusts up through the backing and leaves one loop produced. As the rug is worked on, with the rug pile uppermost, it is possible to see the work as it "grows"—this eliminates the necessity of turning the rug over every few moments to see how the design has progressed.

The needle works in any direction, a slight turn enables any pattern to be followed, thus making the continuous turning of the rug unnecessary.

PRINTED BY : CHARTER PRESS (RHUDDLAN) LTD., GREAT BRITAIN

IT IS a point worthy of note that the time spent in producing a valuable and artistic Rug (which may be worked in colours suited to its surroundings), is no more than that occupied in work of often quite indifferent merit.

Nothing can be more suitable, or better appreciated, for a Wedding or Birthday Present, than one of these Rugs, which with fair wear will last a lifetime.

For Bazaars.

Most Bazaar Holders know the difficulty of getting something new, that has really an element of novelty in it. By one's own exertion, an Eastern stall, similar to those seen every day in Bazaars of the Eastern Cities, can be produced at a small cost and prove quite an attractive feature; the rugs, etc., meeting with the readiest sale.

For Schools.

Many Teachers are anxious to adopt occupations which do not require too much attention, and at the same time are educational and useful. Rug-making is an admirable occupation for girls and boys, and in mixed schools the occupation is exceptionally applicable, because the boys can be employed in the preparation of the material, such as cutting and sorting of the wools.

The Rugs and Mats when finished are very durable and find a ready sale, and the money so derived can be applied to further purchase of material.

For Unions and Infirmaries.

Rug-making is a pleasure for the infirm, aged, or bedridden inmates, and work calculated to beguile many a weary hour, and to add zest to their lives.

For Sailors.

No pastime is more popular on board His Majesty's Ships than Rug-making. We have seen many specimens of Rugs made by Sailors, of excellent workmanship and design, in fact many of them surpassing Turkish and Persian rugs, and no doubt giving much pleasure to the wives and mothers who eventually receive them as gifts.

KINDLY KEEP THIS LIST FOR FUTURE ORDERING.

11

Testimonials.

A few of thousands of Testimonials received by W. Jones & Co.

Twenty years ago Miss Tennant made a Kneeler and Chancel Rugs for the Church here. Those carpets and rugs are still in existence and as good as new.

The Door-mats I made over **twenty-five years ago** from your Thrums are still in constant use, and will wear for many years yet, and I am anxious to get some more of the same material.

Yours sincerely,
ANNIE ROBINSON

Goods received, and I am delighted with the quality of both Wool and Canvas.

Yours truly,
N. BUNKER.

Several Rugs made from your materials have been in hard wear for **over twenty-five years,** and are still in good condition.

Yours truly, BESSIE THOMPSON.

Your Wools are most satisfactory, they make beautiful Rugs, equal to those made in Turkey
Yours faithfully,
ADA ELLIS.

Many thanks for Wool Waste and Canvas received this morning. I am much obliged to you for the splendid quality you have sent which gives entire satisfaction.
Yours faithfully,
H. COOKE.

FORTY YEARS AGO W. Jones & Co. introduced Rug-making by hand, **thousands of Rugs made then are still in wear,** and the materials they now supply are of the same quality. We caution ladies against buying cheap shoddy wools now on the market, many imported from the Continent—our goods are produced in Britain by British labour.

10

A latchet hook

In Newfoundland in the 1890s Dr.Wilfred Grenfell founded a mission serving British immigrants in villages along the coast. He remarked that rug hooking was a thriving tradition in the fishing community and the Grenfell Mission developed a flourishing industry hooking pictorial rugs, from dyed strips of silk stockings, which were sold in Canada, America and even in England.

*Vintage hooky rug from Newfoundland (probably 1930s). 76 x 46cm (30 x 18in). ***

> *A clootie ganzie was a smock - a cloth jumper*
> Durham

In Scottish fishing communities, woven straw mats were called 'flatties' which preceded 'clootie mats' made from rags. Fishermen's families in Britain also knitted 'Ganzeys' (Guernseys) the traditional thick, woollen sweaters worn at sea. Individual villages had their own patterns, with variations for different families. If the body of a drowned fisherman was found, it could be identified by the pattern on his ganzey. (The woman who told me this remembered it from her childhood in Ireland.)

*Vintage prodded slip mat. Woollens 60 x 46cm (26 x 18in).***

> *My mum used to make the big, long ones and we kids had to cut the pieces. It was a case of get it done or we've nothing to eat: it was our livelihood.*
> West Midlands

Red cloth was greatly prized for rag rugs as poor people's clothes were mostly dark in colour. A common design feature was a red diamond known as the 'devil's eye': if a passing devil looked down your chimney and saw the devil's eye on your hearth rug, he knew there was already a devil in the residence and moved on. (This story has been told to me by both house dwellers and narrow boaters).

Variations on the devil's eye theme. Woollen rugs progged by the author. Private collections

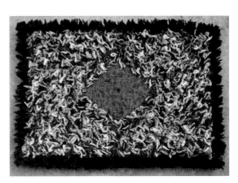

152 x 76cm (60 x 30in) progged rug for a narrow boater who asked for a circle instead of a diamond. Rag rug making was one of the traditional skills practised by narrow boaters.

Progged rug 75 x 50cm (30 x 24in)

Before central heating, when houses were draughty, rag 'slip mats' were laid across the doors. During the second world war, when cloth was scarce in the UK, people still managed to make rag rugs, even in the air-raid shelters.

> *My mum wouldn't leave the rag rug set up by the fire when the sirens went. She'd get us all in the shelter and carry on making the rug.*
> Liverpool

Vintage proddy from Liverpool

> " *I used to lie in bed counting the bombers going out and try to stay awake to count them coming back. I knew from the sound of the engines what type of 'planes they were. All the kids in the village just worked. They needed all hands to get the harvest in. Saturday/Sunday we just picked peas (dig for victory). I pegged my skirt into a rug and got a hiding. Eventually I pegged it all into the rug. There was no new skirt. 'Don't you know there's a war on?' they said.* "
> Nr. Evesham

Women mat making at Willington, with Mrs H C Coates on right. Beamish Museum

Born of necessity, and associated with poverty, rag rug making declined in more affluent times in the UK until it reappeared briefly in the 1960s, and again, in the 21st century, when the "make do and mend" ethos has been revived. With the variety and abundance of textiles we have today, recycling has become an art form (upcycling) and people are keen to learn how to revive thrifty, traditional handcrafts as a way to find a quiet, creative space in a frantically busy world. There is a timely, increased awareness of lifestyle choices with low environmental impact.

**Rugs from the collection of Eileen Scholes

REFERENCES:

'Rug Hooking in Maine 1838-1940' by Mildred Cole Peladeau (Schiffer Publishing Ltd. 2008)
'Silk Stocking Mats' by Paula Laverty (McGill-Queen's University Press 2005)
'Weaving Contemporary Rag Rugs' by Heather L.Allen (Lark Books 1998)
'Women's Work: The First 20,000 Years' Elizabeth Wayland Barber (WW Norton & Co. 1994)
The Stroudwater Textile Trust
www.fishingarts.co.uk
www.maineantiquedigest.com
www.makingthemodernworld.org.uk
www.museumoflondon.org.uk
www.oldandinteresting.com
www.spartacus.schoolnet.co.uk
Wikipedia
www.worldtimelines.org.uk

RUG YARNS
some recollections

When people see me making rugs at different events, they often tell me of their early rag rug experiences, which you can see here, and scattered through this book. 'Mat' and 'rug' were names used in different parts of the country; I have used them both.

> *I was born at the beginning of the war. I came from the Forest of Dean. My father was a coal miner down with the pit ponies. We knew real poverty. I remember my mother and grandmother making rag rugs. We had cardboard on the flag stones and sacks. There was thick ice on the insides of the windows – we used to put rags along the bottom. My father worked on a farm and when he had his accident they sacked him and threw us out of the tied cottage with the furniture on the road. We were two girls and four boys. My father cycled round frantically trying to find somewhere we could live.*
> Worcestershire

World War 2 Day at Berrington Hall, Herefordshire.

Enthusiasts standing by a banner made from recycled materials by members of Age Concern, North Herefordshire, with Jenni Stuart-Anderson for Home Front Recall, part of Veterans Reunited Lottery programme to commemorate the 60th anniversary of the end of WW2.

Vintage proddy mat, bought by Eileen Scholes in an antique shop in Cumbria: "The old rugs probably came out during the outbreak of 'foot and mouth', to be soaked in disinfectant at farm gates" (Cumbria was the worst affected area in the outbreak of the disease in 2001 when footpaths were closed in the UK)

" I was evacuated in the war because I lived near the docks in London. We went on a train to Sheffield: 300 children, and the day we did, that's when they bombed Sheffield. We couldn't get off the train and when we did, we were ostracized because they said the bombers had followed the train. In Sheffield the houses were built round a square and they used to sit outside the back doors making rag rugs. They got the leftovers from the mills. My mother made rugs with a dark border which she cut off my dad's black coat. Every year it got   2 inches shorter – she sewed it up so he didn't know! "

Black bordered, hooked rag mats. Beamish museum

Above: Hooky mat, probably made in early 1900s
152 x 84cm (60 x 37in)
Right: Made by Thomas William Richmond of Stanhope, in the 1950s.
100 x 85cm (39 x 37in)

" Grandma Smith used to do that. She'd get up at 4am to get her husband off to work in the steel mill in Sheffield then she'd sit and peg a rug until it was time for the children to get up. She was my mother-in-law. She's been dead 40 years. "
2007

" Rag rugs! Reminds me of our village post-woman when I was a child. She used to make rugs and sell them to buy drink: she was always drunk but she never fell off her bike and always delivered the post on time. "

Hooked rag mat. Beamish Museum

" My grandmother would take the clothes off yer back to do it. 'Has she grown out of that?' She'd say, 'cause I need a bit of red'.
Yorkshire

" We had a neighbour who allowed children in the house – you didn't play inside (it wasn't done – the houses were too small). And we all helped her make a rug. We used to play singing games while we were doing it. She had a couple of her own kids. We loved it. You'd get bored outside. "
Dewsbury

Prodded rug, 137 x 92 cm (54 x 536in), Collection of Liz Turner at the Thomas Shop, Powys

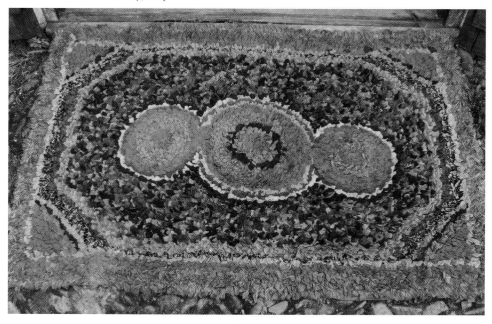

" My brother and sister tipped a pail of water over one (rag rug) and took their shoes and socks off and said they'd made a paddling pool. We lived on the marshes, miles from anything and my mum had to fetch all drinking water in pails and bottles. "
Norfolk

Two vintage hooked rugs at Nantwich Museum, Cheshire

84 x 44cm (37 x 17in)

93 x 53cms (36½ x 21in)

More Rag Rugs **21**

Two hooked rag rugs made during the war by Les Millman of Selsey, who had been shown rug hooking by a Canadian woman staying next door. Some recycled garments and possibly mill samples – Ebley Mill was still productive but had probably gone on to war work. Donated by Mrs Millman to the Museum in the Park, Stroud, Gloucestershire.

114 x 84cm (45 x 37in)

> *We were so poor we couldn't even afford proper hooks. I can't believe people are still doing it – it was a punishment*

113 x 69.5cm (44½ x 27in)

> *I'm from Rhymney and my dad used to make rag rugs; he was a miner and could do lots of things. Just after the war we used to get clothes parcels from relatives in Canada who had done well for themselves. He would make the rugs out of the clothes we couldn't use.*
> South Wales

Two rugs in Pontypool Museum, Wales. The Welsh dragon rug was donated by her daughter, when the maker died, and was made in the mid 20th century, although it looks more recent.

Progged rag rug 94 x 40cm (37 x 16in)

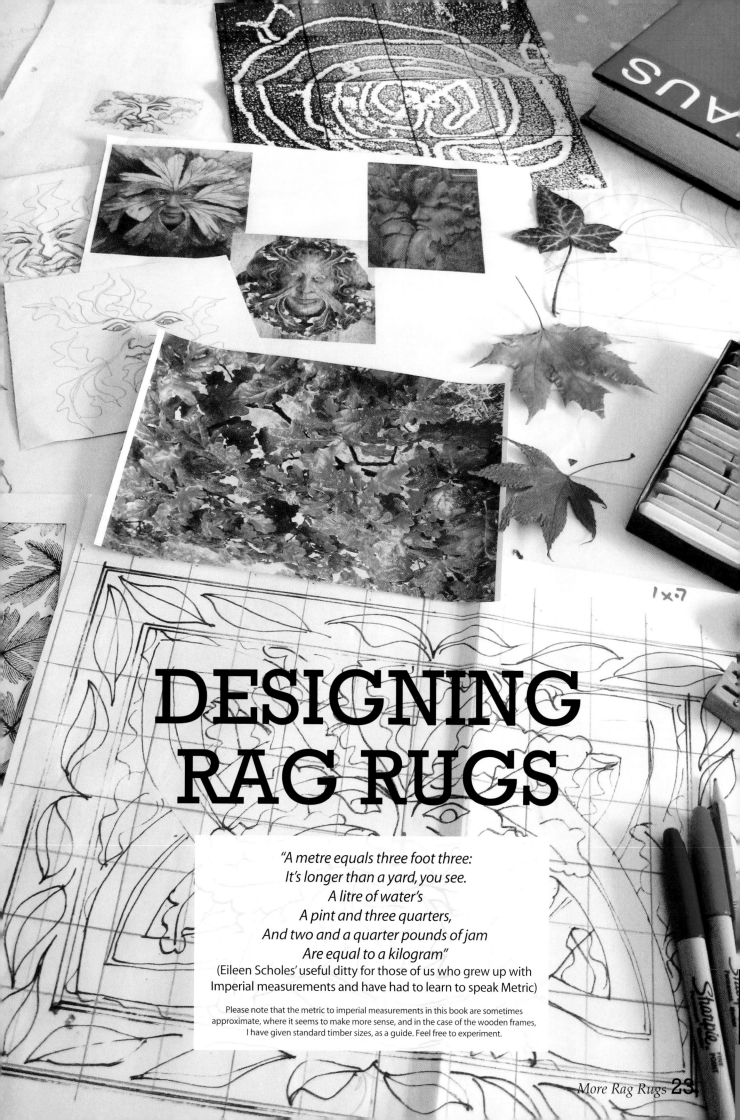

DESIGNING RAG RUGS

*"A metre equals three foot three:
It's longer than a yard, you see.
A litre of water's
A pint and three quarters,
And two and a quarter pounds of jam
Are equal to a kilogram"*
(Eileen Scholes' useful ditty for those of us who grew up with
Imperial measurements and have had to learn to speak Metric)

Please note that the metric to imperial measurements in this book are sometimes
approximate, where it seems to make more sense, and in the case of the wooden frames,
I have given standard timber sizes, as a guide. Feel free to experiment.

DESIGN CONSIDERATIONS

Sometimes it's a question of what you can make with the tools or materials which are available – or even what you can do in the available time. You might want to make something to go in a specific place or to fit into a colour scheme. Where it will go will influence the choice of materials: for example a floor rug which will get plenty of traffic should be made from woollen fabrics as they wear better than, say, cottons which would be more suitable for a bedroom rug (unless your bedroom is very cold). A rug for a bathroom will get wet so square-holed rug canvas would make a more suitable backing than hessian which smells musty when it gets damp.

If you are making a wall hanging you can mix fabrics and even stitch on additional embellishments like beads, sequins, feathers – anything goes, if it enhances your project.

If you are not sure which materials would work best for your idea, make a small sampler to try different techniques and fabrics. They usually look quite different once they are cut and hooked, progged or plaited. Another way is to make a line drawing, make copies and colour them in different combinations to see what works best (some people do this on a computer). Henri Matisse used to move coloured shapes around to find the arrangement he preferred.

If you don't have a design in mind or don't feel ready to do your own, you could make one of the projects in the book. Experimenting with different fabrics and yarns will give you ideas for future projects. Remember, enjoying the process of making is the most important bit. Making something with your hands can be very relaxing and therapeutic. Even if you use a design by someone else, the choices you make of colours and textures of fabrics will still make it your own unique piece.

> **❝** *I measured the door and made my mat the same width then when I made it and put it down I couldn't open the door – the mat was too thick!* **❞**

After I made version 1, below, I experimented by changing the emphasis of shapes by moving the colours around on the second version. The motifs were inspired by the Art Deco movement.

'Kind of Blue' hooked rugs by the author. Woollens, including hand-spun natural fleece.
94 x 65cms
(37 x 25½in).

Version 1

Version 2
Private collection

DESIGN INSPIRATION

I collect postcards and interesting pictures, ripped from magazines, and sometimes make little sketches of ideas or things I think could inform a design. I take photographs of patterns and collect leaves, shells or bits of fabric which either spark an idea or could be cut up to make a rug. A piece of fabric can be the starting point for a rug; either its colour, texture or interesting weave - I just love tweeds! I look at museum collections, exhibitions of fine art, sculpture, posters and textiles both ancient and modern.

Nature is an endless source of inspiration from flowers and animals to the play of light through leaves or the spiral patterns which occur in so many places. Collect things you like the look of even if you can't use them now: they could be the inspiration for a rug or hanging when the time is right. Observing what is around you helps to build a visual vocabulary which you can draw on for your creative work. The more you work with colours and textures, the more visually aware you become.

I have made quite a few rugs and hangings based on mythology and symbols. I felt for a long time that I would like to make a rug inspired by a crop circle and, finally in 2010, a formation appeared at Old Sarum in Wiltshire, and I thought - that's the one. I combined it with a little silhouette of a horse I had in my collection, to make a mixed technique wall hanging.

So many women say to me that they are no good at art but I think we can all put fabrics together and make something. Our grandmothers didn't worry whether the rug was artistic – they had a sense of achievement from having made something useful with the family's old clothes. Don't be attached to the outcome – sometimes the finished result will differ from what you intended but you can use it as a stepping stone to the next piece you create. The more you do it the better it gets!

Mixed technique hanging by Jenni of
crop formation near Old Sarum, May 2010.
Woollens. 85 x 65cm (33½ x 25½in)

Inspirational
images from
my collection

A georgette handerchief which belonged to author's mum

Inspiration - Art Deco

When I found an eau-de-nil coloured blanket in a charity shop, I thought the colour was perfect for Art Deco inspired rugs; then I found an orange blanket which seemed just right for something inspired by Claris Cliff.

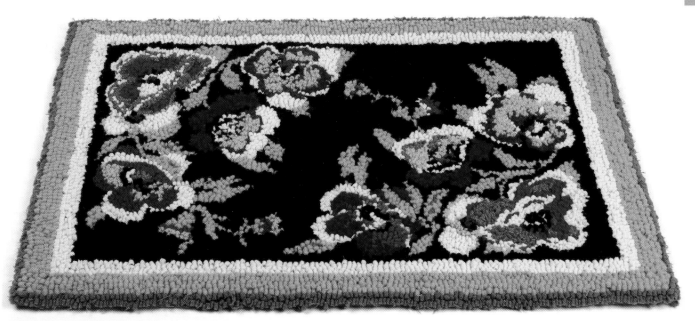

Rug hooked by the author.
Wool jumpers, blankets, yarn. 90 x 65cm (3½ x 25½in)

" *You couldn't buy tea towels. My mother used to wash and unpick flour sacks, then she embroidered a border on them.* "

Rugs I hooked, inspired by the Art Deco work of English ceramicist Claris Cliff. Private collections.

Woollens, 90 x 65cm (35 ½ x 25½in)

Woollens, 90cm diameter (35½in)

COLOUR

The people who made rag rugs years ago, usually did not have much choice of fabrics, just their worn clothes which could not be mended and patched any more. The colours were mostly dark and a little red material would be used for a diamond shape in the middle of a rug, if they could get it. The traditional way was to use whatever came to hand in a fairly random way and you might choose to make rugs that way.

However, now that we have such a choice of materials we can think about how we want to use colour in our rug designs. Here are some basic principles for using colour and a system which will enable you to devise effective combinations.

Sir Isaac Newton developed a circular diagram of colours in 1666 and the colour wheel is a simple system used in the textile trades and by artists.

White light is composed of the colours seen in a rainbow, when it passes through raindrops and separates into the visible spectrum. Black and white are not considered colours: an object appears black if it absorbs all the white light, and white if it reflects all the light.

Key to Colour Wheel:

P = Primary
S = Secondary
T = Tertiary

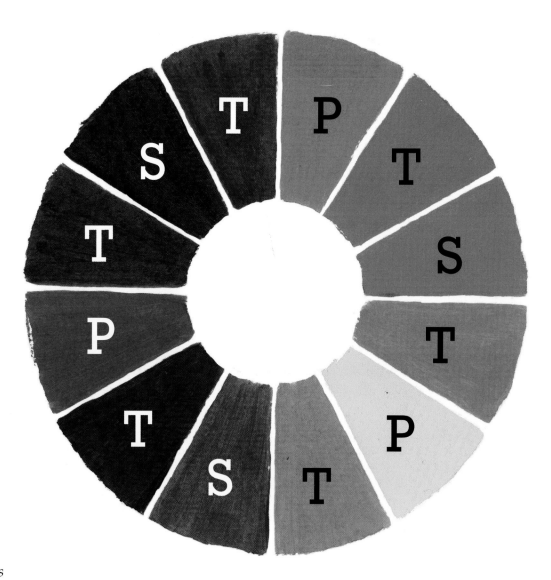

Colours are defined by various qualities known as: hue, value, intensity and temperature.

Hue is the basic quality by which we define a colour: red, blue etc. The **primary** colours (red, yellow, blue) are the ones from which all other colours are derived and which cannot be made by mixing any other colours. The **secondary** colours result from mixing two primaries; they are orange (red + yellow), green (blue + yellow) and purple (blue + red). **Tertiary** colours are mixtures of a primary and its adjacent secondary; they can be described as yellow-orange, red-orange, purple-blue etc.

Complementary colours in nature

Opposite colours on the wheel are called **complementaries**: they are red/green, orange/blue, yellow/purple. Seen together, complementary pairs intensify each other, but can also be used to balance each other in different values and intensities.
Colours next to each other on the colour wheel are called **analogous** – eg red and orange, blue and green.

The **value** of a colour depends on the amount of black or white in it, which determines its lightness or darkness. Light values are known as tints; dark values are called shades.

The **intensity**, or **saturation**, is the purity of a colour – how bright or dull it appears.

Temperature refers to how warm or cool a colour appears. Warm colours (those in the red/yellow range) can seem to advance towards the viewer or make an area appear larger, whereas cool colours (in the blue/green range) seem to recede and appear smaller.

A colour seen in isolation will look different next to other colours, so you can affect the way a colour appears depending on what you use next to it, as you can see below:

The rug technique you use and the texture of a fabric will both affect how that fabric reflects or absorbs light, and therefore how the colour appears. When you decide on a range of colours, gather the fabrics together and try them in different juxtapositions. The appearance of a fabric can be modified depending on the rug technique; progging softens the look of a patterned fabric and ripping cottons instead of cutting them does the same.

Some people make a coloured drawing of their design and then find the rags to match it. Having selected some fabrics, I usually start with an outline of a design and modify it as I go, depending on how the fabrics look together. Sometimes, while I'm working on a rug, I decide to add a touch of a complimentary colour, or an extra line in a border, which is an organic way of making rugs, in the tradition of rag rug making. It really depends on the design and which fabrics I can get. I can also work in a more precise way, developing a design, when it is appropriate. I do apply the ideas outlined in this section , but I also welcome the unexpected.

TRANSFERRING AN IMAGE

Enlarging using a grid system

You could use this method to enlarge an image directly onto the hessian, using one colour marker pen for the grid, another colour for the drawing (try red), and a third (try black) for the final drawing including any corrections. Or, if you need to reverse the image for working with a speed shuttle, enlarge it using this method onto tracing paper first, then flip it over before you draw round the image, using it as a template – in which case you won't need to draw the grid on the hessian.

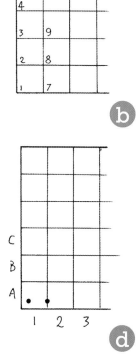

How to do it

To work one of the rug designs from this book, you can enlarge it using a grid; we'll use the Celtic Knot design on page 77 as an example (a). Look carefully at the template and check how many squares there are in the grid, both vertically and horizontally: you need to reproduce this grid full size (the size of your rug), so make sure you have a large enough piece of paper. For this design you need 8 squares one way, and 6 squares the other. Now draw the grid on your piece of paper, making every square the same chosen size. Number the squares to identify them, on both template and your new grid; either give each square a number (b), or use numbers across the bottom, letters up the side (c).

Look at the first square – we'll begin at the bottom left-hand square of the design, but you can choose where to start – and note where the corner is: make a dot there. Now note where the border line crosses the grid square and make another dot (d). Then, make another dot where the line crosses the next box. So follow the line and make a dot where it crosses each line of the grid (e). Then you just join the dots to create your line.

On a straight line like this border it's easy, and you follow exactly the same process with curved lines as well, as shown in (f) and (g).

It really is easier to do than it sounds. I was amazed the first time I tried it at how like the original my scaled up copy was.

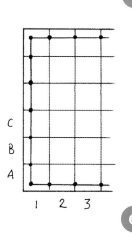

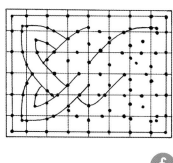

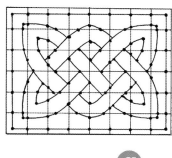

You may want to use this system to enlarge an image you have chosen from another source. Decide on the overall finished size of your rug and how big you want the image to be inside it.

If you want to preserve the original image (a photograph, for instance) scan it or take a photocopy. Measure the height and width of the image and divide by 10 to give you the size of the boxes for the grid, which you can draw over the image in pencil.

To draw a grid on the image copy: measure the width of the image and divide by two, to find the centre. Draw a vertical line through the centre. Measure the height of the image, divide by two and draw a horizontal line through the centre (h). Divide the width of the image into round increments: for instance if the rug will be a metre (round up to 40in) wide, that divides neatly into 10cm (4in) widths.

Working out from the centre lines, which form a cross, draw a grid with boxes the same size (i). Now follow the instructions in the preceding section to enlarge and transfer the image.

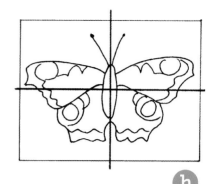

h

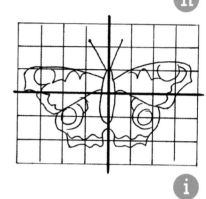

i

Enlarging using a photocopier

Trace the image first so you have a simplified line drawing. Decide on the finished size of the rug (measurement A). Measure the image (measurement B) and divide A by B to get the enlargement ratio. For example, if a rug is to be 1metre (100cm) wide and the image measures 20cm: 20 goes into 100 five times, so the image needs to be enlarged to five times its size, or 500%. (Or, without the maths, just keep enlarging it until the size looks right. You may need to tape photocopies together until it looks big enough).

Tips on enlarging:
- Greaseproof kitchen paper makes good tracing paper and you can tape bits together if necessary.
- If you are enlarging something complex (like a person or an animal) from a picture, trace the outline of it first so you then enlarge that simplified line drawing. Draw lines round areas of shadow etc.
- Remember to flip your tracing over if you are working from the back for a speed shuttle to work a mirror image.

You can see the grid in red used for a complex design, reversed to work from the back with a speed shuttle

The finished hanging, mounted on black fabric. Collection of Helen Smith

MATERIALS
TOOLS &
EQUIPMENT

> " There was an old saying: 'What you doing?
> I'm pegging a rug' - meaning mind your own business. "
> Yorkshire

MATERIALS

Once you start making rag rugs you look at fabrics in a different way – "What a lovely coat" you say, thinking how good it might look in your next rug! Once family and friends hear about your new obsession (sorry, hobby), they might well offer you their cast-off clothes. Charity/ thrift shops have items too tatty to display which they may sell you cheaply, if you ask. Jumble sales and car boot sales can be a source of inexpensive old clothes suitable for rag rugs. Matted sweaters make good strips for hooking; curtains, blankets and sheets provide larger amounts of a single colour for projects. Most women seem to have a stash of fabrics or sewing off-cuts, or you could weed out clothes you never wear and breathe new life into them as rugs.

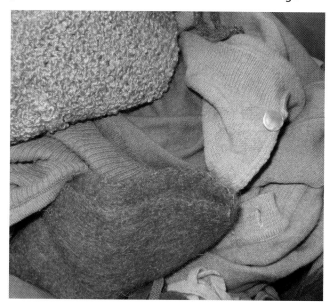 

As you try different fabrics for different techniques you will probably find you prefer some for one technique, some for another. Try working small samples in different techniques and materials and save them as a reference sampler for projects later.

How much material?

If you need to calculate how much fabric you will need for a specific area, measure a square of fabric, cut it up and hook or prog it into some hessian (burlap). Then you can multiply that amount by the number of times it would fit into the area you want to cover.

I prefer to estimate by eye and rag rug makers in the past just used another shade or colour when they ran out of the one they were using. The results can be really quirky. You can also blend shades of a colour (see backgrounds page 73). You learn to judge whether a garment will be enough or how to modify your original idea by improvising with what you have, which I think of as organic design! Often, on workshops, people say they haven't quite enough of a colour to finish the border so I suggest taking out every fifth or tenth piece and replacing it with a different shade.

Alternatively, you can prog a short line, say 15cm (6in), count the number of pieces, measure your border and divide it by 15cms x the number of pieces.

Stripes: one way of spreading some interesting fabric, like tweed, across a rug, by interspersing it with plain fabric, like a blanket. Progged rug by the author. Woollens 87 x 48cm (34 x 19in). 25½in)

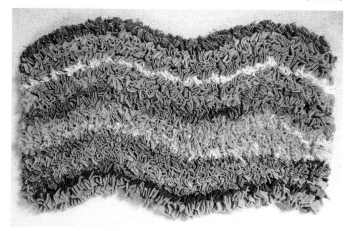

For hooking I like to use sweaters because they have a spring and resilience which makes them fluff out so they fill the area better than thinner materials. Medium and lightweight machine knits hold together better than loose hand knits: if the strip breaks when you tug it gently then the strip is too narrow, or it probably is not suitable for hooking.

Types of Rags

Most fabrics can be used for progged rugs and in bygone days they used everything they could get, all mixed together. I like to use woven fabric for progging, like dress cottons, curtains, woollen skirts, jackets, and blankets. I tend to use similar fabrics in a single piece, so they wear and wash in the same way, but other makers mix all sorts and I am becoming less of a purist! Any pattern in the weave or on the surface of the fabric will look blurred and impressionistic when it's been cut up and progged in. Checks, stripes, tweeds all look very different progged and provide visual/textural interest; strong prints become muted by the process. Fabrics which are printed on one side look softer in colour too, as you will also see the unprinted side in the mix.

Fair Isle or patterned jumpers produce interesting effects, as do tweeds. Velvet or needlecord add richness to any mix and sweat-shirts, T-shirts and patterned kids' clothes can be brightly coloured, easy to get and they hook/prog well. I mix plain and printed cottons and sometimes add some silk, net, synthetics or glitter fabric if it enhances a particular piece. For plaited rugs I collect textiles with an appealing surface colour and/or texture, and I have used dress fabric, leaving the lace sewn on it for textural interest.

A BIT OF THIS BLUE WILL DO!

If you collect fabrics you like, you might not use them for a rug but you could copy a motif or colour combination which works well. Unusual fabrics from faraway places can offer inspiration; chiffon scarves and coloured tights could all enliven a project but the most hardwearing woollen fabrics are best for a floor rug. Knitting wool hooks well and I am delighted with the look of hooked, hand-spun sheeps' wool. As spinning is so labour intensive I eke out such precious yarn by using strips of blanket in the same piece.

Rug hooked by author. The background is contour hooked with cream wool and some hand spun yarn.

Storing Rags

I fold cottons and synthetics on shelves: if you have the space, it's visually stimulating to have beautiful fabrics around. I like to separate woollen items into different colours – it makes it easier to find a particular shade. The materials I am currently using, I keep in a large basket which I move to where I am working.

To protect woollens from clothes moths I spray them a bit with essential oils in water (lavender, citronella and mint) and store them in transparent plastic boxes or bags. I had an infestation of tiny moths which ate my wool and I used essential oils and pheromone traps. Putting woollies in plastic bags in a freezer stops moth eggs from hatching.

Preparation

I wash rags before I store them but I don't try to mat (felt) sweaters as new wool has been treated against shrinkage, and cast-off woollen clothes are usually felted by the time I get them. You could cut them before storing them, as my teacher did, but I cut them as I need them. (The sizes I use for different techniques are covered under those sections; see page 39 for cutting techniques). If the fabrics are very creased, ironing them before cutting up makes it easier to cut straight pieces.

If you are using hessian (burlap) sacks, you could steam iron or wash them before use to get rid of any moth eggs. When you are ready to set out your rug draw the outline with a marker pen leaving a seam allowance of 10cm (4 inches) around the outside and use a ruler: don't follow the weave which is not always straight.

June Emmerson's tidy store of pegloomed rugs and materials

Eileen Scholes' well organized workroom

BASE/GROUND FABRICS FOR RAG RUGS

Sacks

If you can get jute sacks, they make good backing fabric. Sometimes, if you unpick the stitching along the sides, that reveals two selvedges and you can work right up to the selvedge having folded the other two short edges over to the top before you start, working through those two layers. Bird peanuts and coffee beans still come in sacks in the UK but easier to find is:

Hessian

I use natural 10oz common jute upholstery hessian (burlap) for hooking and progging. I have occasionally used coloured hessian when the backing might be seen but it is usually a closer weave so harder to poke the tools into, but if I need a rug to be machine washable I use open-meshed white rug canvas.

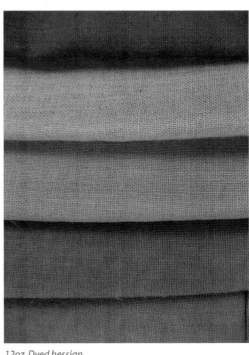

Natural 10oz common hessian

12oz. Dyed hessian

Rug Canvas

Comes in different widths and numbers of holes per inch. Craft and needlecraft suppliers sell it and it is usually stiff with starch (to facilitate latchet hooking without a frame). It softens with use and washing but is more expensive than hessian. If hessian makes you sneeze, you might try rug canvas.

Other

I have used linen scrim, doubled, which is softer and more flexible than hessian. In America, many rug hookers use monk's cloth, a cotton basket-weave material.

Rug canvas

Rug canvas which has been used for progging (back view)

Tips on backing:

- Hessian smells when it is damp so would not make a good bath mat backing, but it can be hand washed. I don't usually wash it first but I do wash sacks which have been used for foodstuffs.

- If you need to join two bits of hessian, overlap them by at least 15cm (6in), stitch two lines of stitching parallel to the two edges, then prog or hook through two layers together.

Hessian backing silk screened with terrier design by the author as part of a kit for hooking

The sugar came in 20cwt.sacks and we used to measure and weigh it all out in the shop. The bags were used for the rag mats.

Terrier rug, hooked from back with speed shuttle produces a mirror image.
Mel was a street-wise dog who lived with me after 3 previous owners.

TOOLS

Y ou can make rag rugs with minimal equipment, but there are some specialized tools which make it quicker and easier. Listed below is everything I use to do my project techniques in this book, but some of this equipment is optional. It's always easier to use the right tool for the job and at the beginning of each Technique section you'll find a picture of the appropriate tool along with instructions on how to use it. You will find the sections explaining the individual techniques, and the relevant tools, on the following pages:

prodding : page 45, progging: page 51, hand hooking: page 63, hooking with a speed shuttle: page71, plaiting/braiding: page 79, peg loom weaving: page 93.

Tools I use for making rag rugs: clockwise from right – dressmaking scissors, yew and brass hook, steel hook, speed shuttle, bodger tool for progging, cutting gauge.

Useful Items

When I am making rugs I find the following tools and bits of equipment useful:

- metre rule, yardstick or straightedge to draw edges of design
- tracing paper for transferring designs
- large sheets of paper for drawings of finished designs
- scissors for cutting paper
- sticky tape for joining paper or photocopies
- marker pens for drawing designs on paper and hessian (burlap)
- dressmaking pins
- sharp dressmaking scissors
- needles and threads, for finishing rugs and stitching hessian to a frame
- bodkin for lacing plaited rugs
- staple gun if you use a stretcher or picture frame (see page 41)
- carpet tape for finishing edges (optional, see p.99)
- latex carpet adhesive (optional, see page 99)
- an iron will be useful, sometimes
- sewing machine – not essential but quicker than hand stitching plait strips

Cutting Tools

I cut woven fabrics along the warp or weft threads and I cut machine knitted sweaters in strips, from neck to waist. I also rip cotton fabrics (children enjoy doing this).

> *We used to make them in the war – the bits were the length of a Swan Vesta box and the width the same as the narrow edge.*
> (Swan Vestas were boxes of matches)

Scissors

The satisfying snip, snip sound of good sharp dressmaking scissors has no substitute: it's a whole different experience using blunt ones. I also use a small pair of embroidery or nail scissors to snip off the ends while I'm hooking, but they are not essential.

> *My gran used to put her new rugs down in the summer and her old ones in the winter. Also cut stockings in strips and hooked them – who's cutting the strips tonight?*
> Lincolnshire

Cutting Gauges

Originally used for cutting Turkey rug wool to make rugs with a latchet hook, these gauges also work for long strips of rag. You wind the strip round the gauge, moving along the length of it, then run the scissors along the groove in the side of the gauge, snipping as you go. It's a sort of low tech, mass production technique giving you a number of same size pieces for prodding or progging. Don't wind the strip around only one end of the gauge though, or the fabric will be too thick to cut.

Cutting up a strip of fabric using a cutting gauge

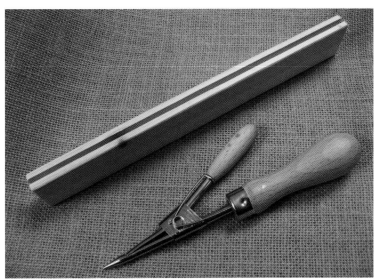

Cutting gauge and bodger for progging

" In the village where I grew up my mum would send the cut bits to Mrs McNally and she'd have a rug for you by tea time. That was in a remote part of Scotland. "

Rotary cutters

A self-healing cutting mat, used with a rotary cutter and a non-slip ruler makes faster work of cutting fabric: you can cut through several layers of fabric simultaneously. The mat and the ruler usually have centimetres and inches marked on them, so you can line the fabric up with the markings. The rotary cutters are extremely sharp, and even though they have a safety lock, they shouldn't be left where children can get hold of them. In fact, a woman told me that she joined a quilting group and the first time she met with them she left her cutter on her mat without engaging the safety lock. They told her not to come back again! Don't use the cutter with an ordinary metal ruler either – the special non slip rulers are much safer.

Cloth stripping machines

If you intend to make a lot of hooked rugs, it is worth investing in one of the cloth stripping machines which cut fabric into strips. I have only seen American ones and my Rigby Cloth Stripping Machine (see pic) has cutter wheels which come in different widths. I use mainly the 3/8in cutter or, when cutting strips of thick matted blankets, I use the 1/4in cutter. First I cut sweaters, or fabric, into manageable sized panels and feed them into the cutter against the guide, turning the handle so that two strips come out the other side (a bit like a pasta machine).

Without a cutter, you can cut the fabric strips side by side using scissors with the fabric flat on a table. It makes a change when you are hooking to stop and cut a pile of strips. Iron any creases out of cottons to make cutting easier and more accurate.

Clockwise from top left: self-healing cutting mat, non-slip ruler, rotary cutter, Rigby Cloth Stripping Machine, dressmaking scissors, pointed scissors, cutting gauge.

Various small frames which can be used for hand hooking

Frames

If the backing material is held taught on a frame it is easier to push in a rug hook and both hands are free if you are not holding the hessian. For hand hooking you could just staple the hessian to a simple frame like a picture frame or use drawing pins (thumb tacks). For hooking relatively small items, an embroidery or needle-point frame works well enough and you can roll the hessian around the rotating ends as they used to do on larger frames in the past. I hand hook with my frame horizontal on the table (held steady with something heavy) with the bit I am working on projecting over my lap. That way, I can hold the hook in one hand and the fabric strip in the other. A frame for hand hooking needs to be narrow enough for you to reach the middle with one hand above and one below (see instructions on page 65).

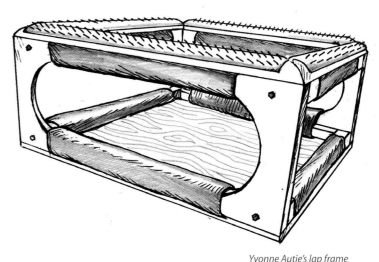

Yvonne Autie's lap frame with gripper strips (could be carpet gripper) to hold the hessian on the top and something smooth covering the wood where she puts her arm inside to hold the fabric strip.
overall dimensions:
16.5 x 43 x 40cm
(6½ x 17 x 16in)

For hooking with a speed shuttle it's essential to stretch the hessian on a large frame (see overleaf). I sit or stand at my frame, turning it upside down if it makes access easier to a particular area. When I am making a project, I like to see the whole thing at once, so I use a frame which adjusts to different sizes. I had extra long uprights made for a rug which was bigger than would fit in my square frame. Large rugs are really heavy, but quite a few people have told me about hooked stair carpets they remember, or ones which covered a whole sitting room!

> We had a frame in the family - the extended family, that is. We used to have it between the sink and the table and sit both sides of it. You were allowed to peg the plain until you were good at it, then you could do the mixed. A real test of expertise was to do the red line. Otherwise they were black and navy. My dad used to work on his knee and didn't like using a frame. Somebody asked him to make a rug and had a frame made for him to do it. Afterwards he cut the frame up and made a stool. Recycling's not new y'know.
> Scotland

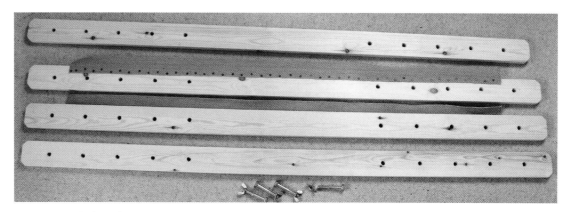

Components of a large frame
4 pieces of wood about 150 x 7 x 2cm (59 x 2¾ x ¾in)
4 M10 bolts appx. 6.5cm (2½in) long. 4 wing nuts to fit bolts
cotton carpet webbing nailed to edge of 2 timber pieces with webbing tacks
holes, large enough for bolts, drilled at approx. 10cm (4in) intervals

A large rug frame suitable for speed shuttle, could only be used horizontally for hand hooking if you can reach the middle of the hessian with your hand beneath frame, i.e. you would need to roll the hessian round the frame if hand hooking a larger rug, thus keeping working area narrow/accessible.

Putting the hessian on a frame

To use a speed shuttle you need to stretch the hessian on a frame: this frame then stands on the floor and leans against a wall while you work. These instructions are for a frame which has webbing attached to two of the pieces; my frame is 1.5m (about 5ft) square. I thread the frame before marking the design on the hessian. Remember that the shuttle pokes the loops into the hessian from the back so you work with a mirror image of your design. For some designs, it doesn't matter which way round you hook it, but with a portrait or writing, you need to reverse the image. To do this, trace the full size drawing, flip the tracing paper over and transfer the reversed image onto the hessian (see transferring an image in Design section).

These instructions for threading a frame are for right-handers; if you are left-handed, reverse the directions when appropriate.

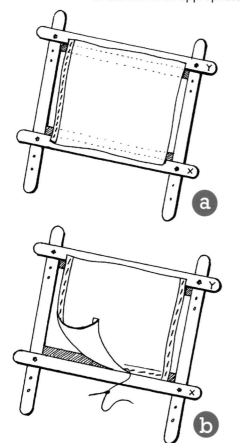

How to do it

1. Lay the frame flat on a table, with the bolts or pegs holding it in a rectangle which allows for the design plus at least 15cm (6in) around the design.

2. Cut a piece of hessian as wide as the aperture formed by the frame, and 10cm (4in) longer at top and bottom, so it overlaps the top and bottom bars (a). Fold over about 3cm (1½in) of the two vertical sides of the hessian, and tack (baste) them with strong thread (b).

3. Slide the frame towards you so that the bottom piece X projects beyond the table about 15cm (6in), and fold the nearest horizontal edge of the hessian over 1cm (½in). Holding the right hand edge of the fold on the frame's webbing (b), stitch the folded edge of the hessian to the webbing, keeping the fold against the frame as you stitch. Work from right to left, using back stitch and strong thread.

4. Before you sew the hessian to the frame at Y it has to be cut to a size which will ensure that it is stretched between sides X and Y. Push the loose end of the hessian under the frame at side Y and, using the inside of Y as a ruler, draw a line on the hessian with a marker pen (c). Cut along this line and fold the edge over 1cm (½in).

5. Slide the frame so that side Y projects beyond the table (I move round to the other side of the table). In order to sew the hessian to the webbing, as you did at side X, you'll need to undo the bolts through side Y and carefully slide Y towards X, just enough to enable you to sew all along the webbing as before (d). Check the measurement between sides X and Y as you go, to make sure they remain parallel while you sew; the stretching won't work properly if they aren't.

6. Now you can put the bolt back on one side of Y. You will find that you need to pull hard to get the other side of Y over the second bolt, which assures that your hessian is stretched taut (d).

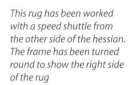

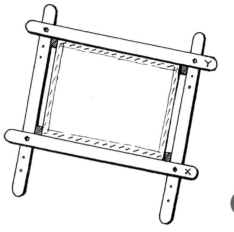

This rug has been worked with a speed shuttle from the other side of the hessian. The frame has been turned round to show the right side of the rug

TECHNIQUES & PROJECTS

This section describes Prodding, Progging, Hooking and Plaiting/Braiding as I do them or have seen them done. There are other ways but these work for me and the other contributors: you might even devise your own way depending on the availability of tools, materials and time, as they did in the past. I was shown Hooking and Progging by Mrs Doris Tunley who made rag rugs for more than 50 years. There is also a project on a peg loom, a more recent innovation for weaving.

For each technique there is a sample project, or more, which you can try and as you gain confidence from having a go, you can make up your own designs. Remember - the people who used to make rag rugs out of necessity probably did not have art training. They learned a technique from family or neighbours and made mats and draught excluders, even carpets to cover whole rooms and stairs!

Dan having a go on Jenni's rug

> **My next door neighbour was a blacksmith and every evening he would sit in a high back chair with a rug over his knees – he would peg one end and me pegging at the other end. I was much slower than him, of course – I was about four. He made the metal pegs himself and his daughter worked in a clothing factory and brought home off-cuts.**
> Warwickshire

PRODDING

A well worn half clothes peg

People used home-made prodding tools – the most common being half a wooden clothes peg, sharpened to a point. I have even seen animal horns which had been used to make mats on remote farms and when the men worked metal, they sometimes fashioned a rug tool from a nail.

Prodding involves literally poking or prodding a small piece of fabric through a base material. This was the most common technique which had different names in different parts of the country: 'pegged', 'pricked', 'clippies', 'proddies', 'stobbies' and, in Scotland, 'clootie mats'.

Fabrics were cut into strips, then into pieces often called 'tabs' or 'lists' and this was frequently the job for the children in the family. I have been told by one person they were not allowed out to play until a certain number had been cut! Another told me they used to play with the tabs under the frame whilst the grown-ups worked on the rug.

" *One way of keeping five children quiet on a winter's night.* "

A hessian sack was usually stretched on a frame and the rag pieces were poked (poke mats) or prodded (proddies) one at a time, from the top, which would be the back of the finished rug. This method gives a shaggy, cut pile and it seems that most people mixed any sort of materials they could get. Several people could sit round a frame prodding together and chat as they worked.

" *In Barnsley market you could buy bits of material ready cut up for pegging a rug but they were expensive. My mother bought a bag but the bits were big so she sewed them together to make a blanket. We had that blanket until we got married.* "
Yorkshire

Rug Prodded by Eileen Scholes, inspired by a painting showing a needlepoint design (1913-14) by Vanessa Bell. Woollen jumpers, 76 x 60cm (30 x 24in)

PRODDING:
How to do it

1. Stretch the hessian on a frame then mark the perimeter of your rug on it leaving a border of 15cm (4in), outside the line, which will form the hem after you finish progging. Mark any design on the hessian. (An alternative way of finishing the rug edges is described in Project 1)

2. Cut or rip the fabric, along the weave, into same sized pieces (tabs), about 7.5 x 4cms (3 x 1½in). You can cut the fabric with scissors or use scissors with an old fashioned cutting gauge, or use a rotary cutter (see page 40).

3. Work along the drawn line (from left to right if you are right handed). With your writing hand, poke a gap between the hessian threads (a) and, using the prodder, poke one end of the tab through the gap receiving it beneath the hessian with your other hand (b).

4. Make a second hole along the line, about a centimeter (½in) away from the first (c), and prod the other end of the tab through it (d). Even up the two ends by tugging them gently beneath.

5. There are two ways you can proceed now:
Single prodding, which spaces the tabs out more and results in a less dense rug; or double prodding, which results in a thicker rug.

For single prodding: leave four or five threads of hessian between the progged tabs, then repeat steps 3 and 4, so there are gaps in the line. Some people just prod the tabs in a fairly random way all over the hessian (children usually do it that way).

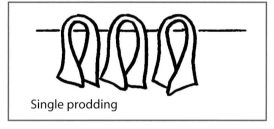

Single prodding

For double prodding: prod the first end of the second tab into the same hole as (d). (This means that every hole has two adjacent tab ends emerging from it (e)). Follow step 3 to finish prodding the second tab and continue along the line so there are no gaps between the tabs. Work the next line parallel with the first, about a centimetre (½in) away from the first line which you worked along the drawn line (that's measured from the centre of one row to the centre of the next row). Work in this way to outline any shape/design you are working in a particular colour. There is no need to stagger the tabs (like bricklaying).

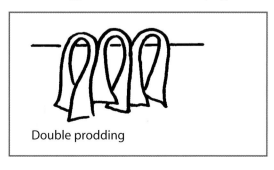

Double prodding

Tips on prodding:

- You may need to vary the width of the tabs depending on the thickness of the fabrics. Cut a couple of pieces first and prog them into the hessian. If they are hard to pull through (thick woollens), cut them a bit narrower. If they slip out when tugged gently (fine cottons), cut them wider. Or use fabrics which are similar and cut tabs the same size.

- If you cut the ends of the tabs diagonally, they will be easier to prod through.

Eileen Scholes finishes prodding

Rug prodded by Eileen Scholes. Woollens from jumble sales. 89cm diameter (35in)

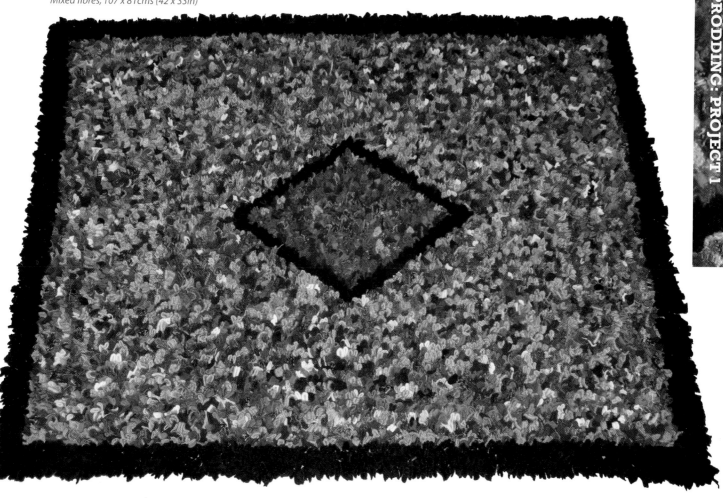

Mizzy mazzy rug made by Eileen for a farmhouse in Cumbria.
Mixed fibres, 107 x 81cms (42 x 33in)

MIZZY MAZZY PEGGED RUG
Project 1 by Eileen Scholes

Eileen Scholes makes rugs using the tool that most people used years ago – half a wooden clothes peg, sharpened to a point. Eileen draws the outline of the rug on the back of the hessian, plus any pattern, like the diamond, then she marks the rug into sections where she writes the date by which each section is to be finished, leaving out any holidays: "It keeps you at it" she says. You could just number the squares and do more than one a day, if you are keen. Mizzy mazzy was a name for a random mixture of fabric pieces – a very common, and practical background for traditional prodded rugs.

YOU WILL NEED:

- hessian, the size of your rug, plus 7.5cm (3in) all round
- a mixture of materials (jumpers, skirts, blankets)
- half a wooden clothes peg, sharpened to a point
- sharp scissors
- marker pen
- sewing machine (optional) or needle and thread
- long ruler
- pins
- needle and thread

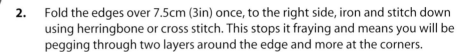

INSTRUCTIONS:

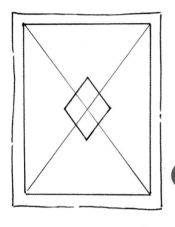

(a)

1. All drawing is on the back, because you peg the rug from the back. On your hessian, draw a rectangle 107 x 81cms (42 x 33in). Placing the ruler from corner to corner diagonally, mark the centre, both ways. This shows you where to draw the central diamond (a). Draw a border line 7.5cms (3in) inside the rectangle.

2. Fold the edges over 7.5cm (3in) once, to the right side, iron and stitch down using herringbone or cross stitch. This stops it fraying and means you will be pegging through two layers around the edge and more at the corners.

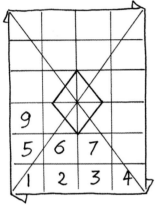

(b)

3. Draw lines which divide the rug into sections about 10 x 7.5cm (4 x 3in) putting the dates by which you want to finish each section, if you want to follow Eileen's example (it works for her). Number them from left to right, starting at one end (b).

4. Cut a mixture of materials into strips no shorter than 5 x 1cm (2 x ½in). For thin materials cut strips a little wider than for thick.

5. With the hessian on the table and the edge where you are starting above your lap, start working from the back. Beginning at the bottom left corner of section 1, twist peg gently to poke a hole between the hessian threads, 1cm (½in) to the right of the corner. Fold the strip lengthwise and poke the end into the hole, receiving the strip with your other hand, beneath the hessian (c). Poke another hole 1cm (½in) to the left of the first hole , then push the other end of the strip into it (d) so you are working along the drawn line from left to right, but each strip has the right- hand end poked in first, then the left.

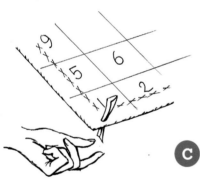

(c)

6. Now poke a hole 1cm (½in) to the right, along the line and poke the end of second strip through it, pushing the left end of it into the first hole you made. This way you have 2 tab ends in each hole which helps to hold them in place and is called double prodding.

7. For the second line Eileen scores the peg along the hessian to mark a straight line parallel to the first line of strips, a centimetre (½in) from centre to centre of the rows. Peg along scored next line, as before, working up the section you want to finish today, line by line.

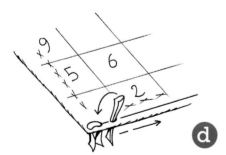

(d)

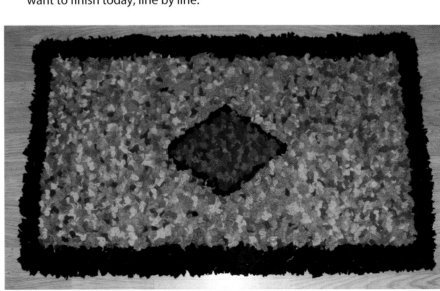

Another mizzy mazzy prodded rug by Eileen Scholes. Mixed fibres, 107 x 81cms (42 x 32in)

PROGGING

A modern 'bodger'
spring clip rug tool

Progged rugs look the same as prodded rugs but are worked from the top, right side up. The fabric pieces (tabs) are pulled through a hessian base with a 'bodger', a spring-clip tool with small jaws. The hessian doesn't need to be on a frame for this technique, in fact it would be difficult to do it on a frame. Although it's possible to prog a picture, the shaggy tabs produce an impressionistic effect so this isn't the most appropriate technique to show details. However, if you do want to prog pictorial detail, use bold, simplified shapes and use contrasting colours to define them.

> *My mother made rugs with a dark border which she cut off my dad's black coat. Every year it got two inches shorter – she sewed it up so he didn't know!*
> East London

Traditionally, progged rugs had a dark border which didn't show the dirt and because there were more dark clothes available. Coloured fabrics were reserved for small details, often a red line or a central diamond, then the rest of the rug was filled in with random mixed pieces which was called 'mizzy mazzy'. There was an abundance of black fabric when Queen Victoria went into mourning for her husband and then at the end of WW2 there was a lot of blackout fabric.

Vintage rug at the Thomas Shop, Wales
Mixed technique, woollens, appx. 46 x 23cm (18 x 9in)

> *That takes me back! Nice to see it. We used tartan kilts to make a tartan design rug: you'd have Royal Stuart in one corner and your Black Watch in another."*
> Edinburgh

Progged rug by the author
Woollens, incl. tartan, 46 x 30cm
(18 x 12in). Private collection

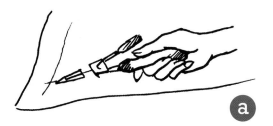

PROGGING:
How to do it

1. Begin progging along an outline of your design. Holding the bodger in your writing hand, poke the point into the hessian and out again about 1cm (½in) further along the drawn line (a).

2. Depress the lever to open the jaws of the bodger and catch the first piece of fabric (tab) by one corner (b).

3. Pull the bodger back out of the hessian, releasing the tab so it stays in the hessian, with its ends sticking out like a bow (c).

4. Poke the bodger back into the last hole it made, where half of the 'bow' sticks up, and out again 1cm (½in) further along the line, as you did in 3. Repeat this process (d), until you have progged one line all around the border or design. Work in lines, parallel to your first line, about 1cm (½in) away, to fill in the shape. No need to stagger the tabs, prog them as they come.

Tips on progging:

- I work from right to left with the backing flat on a table or on my knee so I can hold it steady with my left hand when I pull the tab with the bodger.

- If the progging seems too densely packed and thick, just leave a wider gap between the lines from time to time as necessary. The aim is not to have the base fabric visible from the right side.

- You may need to vary the tab widths if you mix different thickness fabrics. Cut a couple of pieces first and prog them into the hessian. If they are hard to pull through (thick woollens), cut them a bit narrower. If they slip out when tugged gently (fine cottons) cut them wider.

- If you mix fabrics for a floor rug, choose ones which will wash the same and wear the same.

They was on the floor in the day and on yer bed of a night and if you was lucky you got a big one – covered yer feet
Essex

TIP
To stop the hessian fraying whilst you work, you can put masking tape around the edge or sew a zig zag with sewing machine.

STRIPED RUNNER
Project 2 Jenni Stuart-Anderson

Here is a simple design to get you started with a bodger. I worked this rug in woollen fabrics from cut-up coats, jackets and skirts. You could make one the same size or change the length or width to fit the place you want to use it, e.g. make it the width of a hearth. The striped design allows you to use different amounts of fabrics, depending on what you can gather.

TIP
If you need the rug to be an exact size - when you draw the outline of your rug, add 2.5cm for every 30cms (one inch for every foot) to the length/width to allow for "take-up" which means that the progged pieces pull the hessian shorter than when you started. This amount might vary depending on your style of progging, thickness of bits (but, hey – we're hand-making a rag rug and don't want it to look machine made!)

YOU WILL NEED:

- hessian base (ground) fabric at least 80 x 110cm (32 x 44in)
- fabrics or clothes to cut up
- a bodger rug tool
- sharp scissors
- marker pen
- long ruler
- needle and thread
- pins

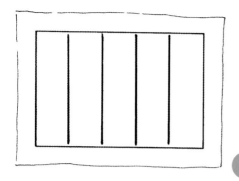

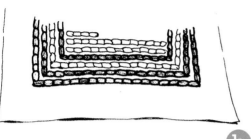

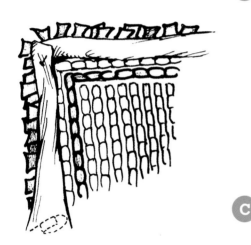

INSTRUCTIONS:

1. Select fabrics of a similar weight, eg coats, skirts, and remove seams, waistbands etc.

2. Draw a rectangle the size of the outside measurement of your finished rug plus an allowance for "take-up" if necessary (see TIP below rug photo.) Draw the outline onto the hessian using marker pen and long ruler, making sure you leave a border of at least 10cm (4in) all round to turn under later. Draw about 4 lines across the rug to give a guide for keeping the lines parallel (a). No need to draw every line, just prog the parallel rows a centimeter (½in) apart, from the centre of one row to the centre of the next.

3. Cut the fabric you will use for the border into pieces about 7cm x 2.5cm (2¾ x 1in) along the weave and prog the first line all around the border, following the instructions on page 53. On the rug in the picture I progged 2 lines of black fabric round the edge, then one in mixed tweed pieces, then another line in black (b). You can work a border the same or make it three or four lines in dark colours (depends how much dark fabric you have).

4. Cut a different coloured fabric into same sized pieces and prog a line or two across the rug, parallel to the border. Now you can see whether you have enough fabric in that colour to work many or few lines. If you have just a little, you can spread a few lines across the rug, filling the gaps with stripes in other shades/colours.

5. When you have progged the whole area inside the outline, turn the rug over and fold the hessian border under twice (c), following the instructions for hemming on page 97.

> *Granny Forbes had sixteen children and she taught my mother to make rag rugs. She was a McKenzie, farming on the outer islands. Her name was Rodina, which we always thought was Scottish but when we researched it, it was Scandinavian.*
> Isle of Lewis

TIP
To stop the hessian fraying whilst you work, you can put masking tape around the edge or sew a zig zag with sewing machine.

Progged runners by the author.

Woollens. 76 x 48cm (30 x 19in)

Woollens, including some Harris tweed 97 x 56cm (38 x 22in). Private collection

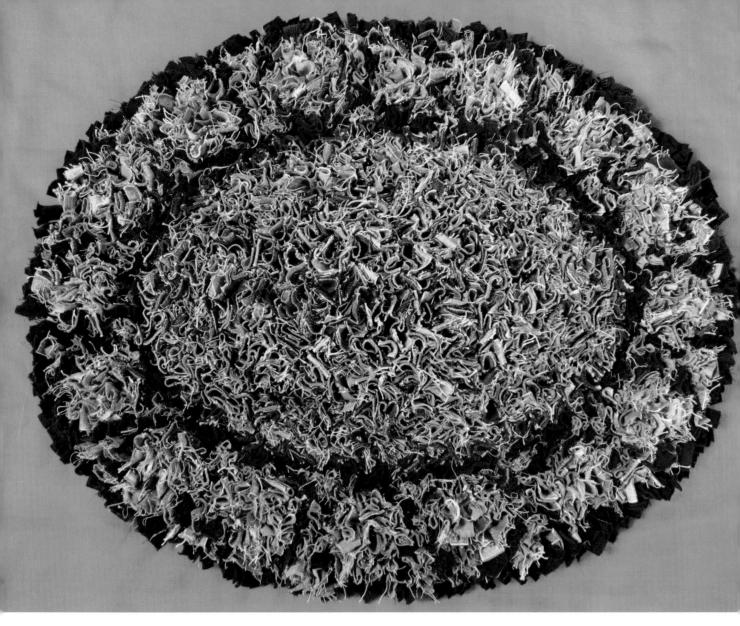

OVAL DENIM PROGGED RUG
Project 3 by Jenni Stuart-Anderson

The rug in the photograph was made from a pair of navy needlecord jeans mixed with a black tee shirt for outlining circles and ovals, filled in with a denim shirt and some jeans.

YOU WILL NEED:
- something oval, and circular, to draw round (or enlarge diagram)
- hessian base fabric the size of your oval plus 20cm (8in) on length and width for the hem
- fabrics or clothes to cut up
- a bodger rug tool
- sharp scissors
- marker pen
- needle and thread
- pins

Rags for upcycling

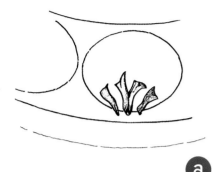

INSTRUCTIONS:

1. Collect 2 or 3 garments in darker colours for outlining and 3 or 4 garments in varying shades for filling in. Fabrics should be of similar weights. Cut off seams and other thick bits.

TIP
You could make this rug using light-weight fabrics, like thin cottons but you would have to cut the pieces wider so they don't slip out.

2. Enlarge the template on page 58 onto the hessian backing, leaving backing as a rectangle until you finish progging. (see instructions on page 30)

3. Cut two test pieces of fabric about 7.5cm (3in) x 2cm (¾in) follow tips on page 53 to test if the size is right for your fabric. Tug a piece gently and if it slips out easily, cut pieces a bit wider. If using thicker jeans, cut pieces a little narrower if they are hard to pull through.

4. Start by progging round the small circles in darker fabric (a) and then round the oval on the inner side of the circles (b) and the oval which will form the outside edge. Using the bodger in your writing hand follow the instructions on page 53.

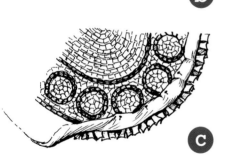

5. Choosing the lightest coloured fabric work parallel circles of pieces next to the darker ones, about 1cm (½in) away, centre of row to centre of row. The contrast will help the darker lines to stand out.

TIP
For this rug I drew round a large oval dish and then drew circles around a yoghurt pot lid. You could do that instead of enlarging the template.

6. Using a mixture of the other shades (not dark), fill in all the gaps with parallel lines of progging.

7. When you have progged the whole area inside the outline, turn the rug over and cut round the outside oval allowing a hessian border of about 6cm (2½in). Fold the hessian edge under twice (c), pin and stitch with thread. (See section on finishing)

Variations on the design: rag rugs by the author
Cottons, approx. 70 x 54cm (27+1/2in x 21in)

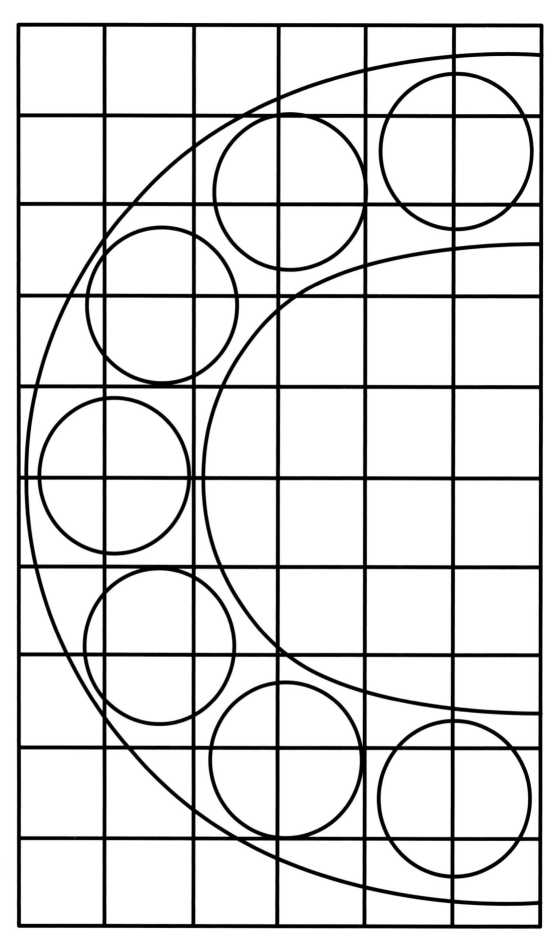

DIAGRAM FOR ONE HALF OF PROGGED OVAL RUG

    We had a new rug every Christmas Eve and I can still smell it (the hessian)
North Yorkshire

TIP
The doorstop
in the photograph was
progged with recycled
cotton pyjamas. As you
are unlikely to wash a
doorstop, you could mix
types of fabric, if
you wish.

This is an easy three dimensional progged project. Basically, you start with a bit of hessian, which you sew into a cylindrical container shape, stuff it, and embellish by progging it with your choice of fabrics.

SHAGGY DOORSTOP

Project 4 by Jenni Stuart-Anderson

YOU WILL NEED:

- hessian at least 86 x 46cm (round up to 34 x 18in)
- quilter's wadding cut to circle, about dinner plate size
- coloured fabrics to prog
- 2 large buttons to decorate
- a bodger rug tool
- sharp scissors
- marker pen
- needle and thread
- pins
- gravel, or similar, to fill door stop for weight
- optional sewing machine

Hessian tube ready for filling, stitching and progging

INSTRUCTIONS:

1. Choose fabrics and, if recycling, remove seams and any lumpy bits.

2. Either trace the circle on page 62 onto paper and cut it out, or draw round a saucer 16cm (approx. 6½in) diameter straight onto the hessian. Draw a rectangle which measures 50 x 20cms (round up to 20 x 8in) on the hessian.

3. Cut out the rectangle, pin and stitch the two short sides together, leaving a seam allowance of about 1cm (½in). This produces a hessian tube. Pin bottom edge of hessian tube to the hessian circle, with seam allowance on the outside, i.e. inside out, and stitch them together, round the circle, leaving seam allowance as before. Now you have a tubular hessian bag .

4. Fold top edge of tube towards outside, 1cm (½in) and stitch round it (a). Turn bag so seams are inside.

5. Take the circle of quilter's wadding and place it inside your bag, covering inside of base, trimming so it stops below folded top edge. Fill with gravel (small stones) to within about 5cm (2in) of top (b), so you can close the top without pulling hessian too tight.

6. Taking opposite sides of top edge, pull them together and pin leaving about a quarter of overall width open on both sides. Stitch sides together between the pins (c). Now close the other opposite sides (d) and stitch.

7. Make a 3 strand fabric plait (braid) about 34cms (13in) long, using 3 fabric strips at least 5cm (2in) wide for strength. (see page 81 for how to plait) Leave about 4cm (1½in) unplaited at each end.

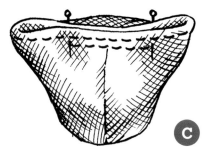

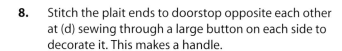

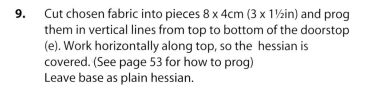

8. Stitch the plait ends to doorstop opposite each other at (d) sewing through a large button on each side to decorate it. This makes a handle.

9. Cut chosen fabric into pieces 8 x 4cm (3 x 1½in) and prog them in vertical lines from top to bottom of the doorstop (e). Work horizontally along top, so the hessian is covered. (See page 53 for how to prog) Leave base as plain hessian.

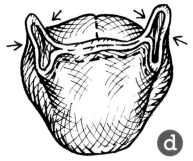

TIP
You could draw round a saucer for the base of doorstop, about 16cm diameter (say 6in).

Piece of thick fabric cut at an angle

A variation, progged with pieces 7cm x 1cm (2¾ x ½in) of woollen blankets in blue, yellow and cream. The pieces were cut with slanted ends

Bolster with removable cover, made by similar method to doorstop, using coloured hessian base and cotton fabric pieces. Cottons, 28cm dia. x 43cm (11in dia x 17in). Progged by Jenni with feather bolster inside

*"Rugs, rugs, rugs.
What about my dinner?"
Lorenzo & Finn
help Jenni at a show*

FULL SIZE TEMPLATE
FOR BASE OF DOORSTOP

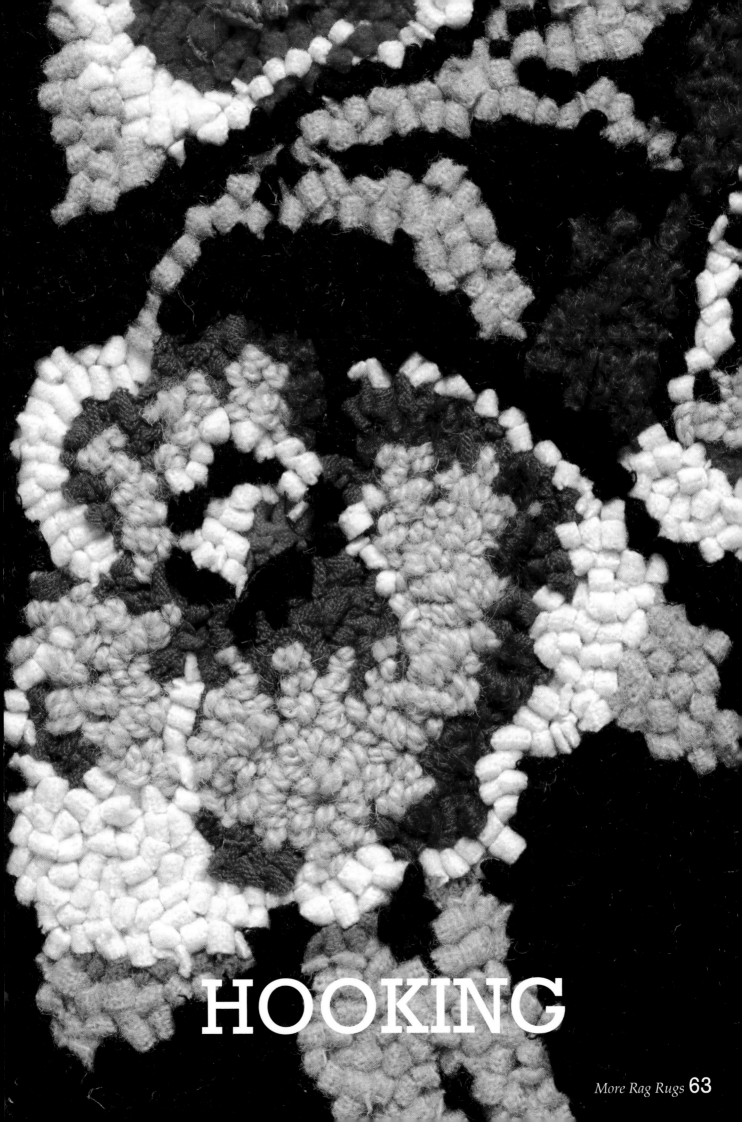

HOOKING

Hooking is the best technique to use if you want to define detail in projects, so for pictures or fine patterns, it works well. Thin strips of fabric are pulled up through hessian (stretched on a frame) to make a series of loops on the top – the right side where the design has been drawn. For hand hooking I work with my frame horizontal on a table, held steady with something heavy, and projecting over my lap. This frees my hands to hold the hook above the hessian in one, and the strip below in the other. You can improvise with a quilting frame, even an artist's stretcher or a picture frame (see page 41). Yvonne used a lap frame for her project 5. Hooking can also be done with a speed shuttle/hook (see page 71). It is quicker than a hand hook, but you need a larger frame and, of course, a speed shuttle.

Hooking with a hand hook

I have found this is easiest with a proper rug hook which fits snugly in your hand and has a shaft which grows thicker towards the handle (unlike a crochet hook). This wider shaft enables you to make a gap between hessian threads large enough to pull a strip through easily, to form a loop on the top.

Rug hooks come in different sizes – many Americans use a small hook for really fine detail. I use a medium rug hook, suitable for strips about 1cm (3/8in) wide, or narrower if the fabric is matted and thick. You can also hook wool (yarn), several strands together, and I use different kinds of yarn alongside woollen fabric strips in a project, sometimes. Experiment! If it looks good – hook it, prog it, or even stitch it!

"Count not the hours but hook for joy" hanging, hand hooked by Eileen Scholes Mixed fibres. 92 x 76cm (36 x 30in)

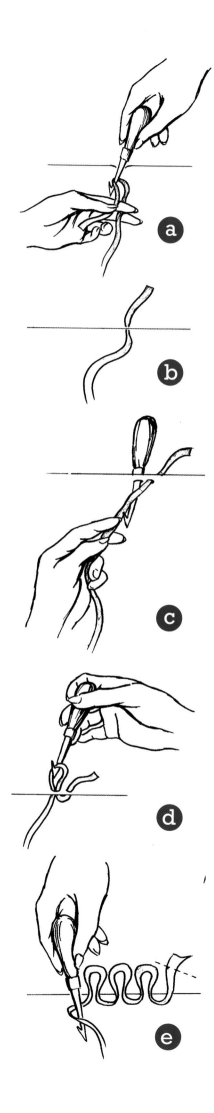

HOOKING:
How to do it

1. Stretch the hessian on a frame and mark your design on it (unless you are rolling it round the frame as you go, in which case, you need to draw it first). Lay the frame so part of the design protrudes over your lap. Begin hooking along an outline of the design, holding the hook in your writing hand above it and holding the fabric strip in the other hand beneath the hessian. Plunge the hook into the hessian on the marked line, inserting it right up to the handle so the wider part pushes a gap between the hessian threads. The hook should face the direction of travel, so you don't pull out the last loop you made. Hook from right to left, if you are right-handed.

2. With your lower hand, loop one end of the strip around the hook (a), release it, then pull the end of the strip to the top of the hessian (b),

3. Two threads further along the line, push the hook into the hessian again; loop the fabric strip around it underneath (c), and pull it to the top, to make a loop (d). Continue along the marked line, creating loops of an even height. When you reach the end of the strip, pull the end to the top and pull the end of the next strip up through the same hole. I trim the strip ends level with the loops as I go.

4. Work round the design outlines, then fill in the gaps with lines of loops leaving about 2 threads between the lines. The aim is to cover the surface with loops. I find it easier to work in parallel lines, which can follow a curve.

> ## Tips on hooking:
> * Using the right tool for the job makes it easier. Although you can bang in a nail with the heel of your shoe, it's more efficient with a hammer! (It took me 2 years to make a rug with a crochet hook before I discovered proper rug hooks – ouch!)
>
> * I notice beginners are often timid about pulling loops up high enough: try 1cm/half inch loops. You could also vary the height of the loops to emphasise different parts of your design.
>
> * Remember to plunge the hook in, don't just pick with the end or it will be hard to pull the loops up. The gap needs to be big enough for a strip of fabric.

WHIRLPOOL GALAXY
Project 5 by Yvonne Autie

This wall hanging was hooked by Yvonne Autie using a portable lap frame and strips of blankets, sweatshirts, cotton, lace curtain, jersey, lace tights, crimplene, stretchy velvet, tee shirts, chiffon, yarn, plastic bags, shoelace, acrylic and woollen jumpers. Yvonne used 8 or 9 different shades of each colour. If she can't find enough colours she takes a selection of white and cream items which contain some natural fibres and dyes them in her washing machine after removing zips, seams etc. The result is a useful collection of different tones of a similar colour which add life and vibrancy to anything she hooks.

TIP
You can make your hanging the same size as Yvonne's or scale it up or down to fit your frame.

YOU WILL NEED:

- 10oz hessian base (ground) at least 67 x 59cm (26x23in)
- a diverse mixture of fabrics
- a frame (see section on frames)
- scissors
- chalk
- marker pens
- a rug hook
- needle and strong thread
- hanging rod

INSTRUCTIONS:

1. Cut a piece of hessian large enough for the design plus a border of at least 7.5cms (3in) to hem later, more if you are not using a lap frame. Machine zig-zag round the edge of your hessian to prevent fraying, or use masking tape on the edge.

2. Attach the hessian to a frame (see page 41/frames). If using a lap frame, position hessian after you have drawn the design on it.

3. Enlarge the diagram on page 68 following instructions on page 30 or draw a rectangle on the hessian 59cm x 51cm (23 x 20in) plus border, and sketch the spiral freehand, using chalk, then marker pen.

4. Cut some strips about 0.6cm (¼in) wide in the colours for the centre of the spiral. Start hooking the centre and work outwards following the curves of the spiral (a) (see page 65/hooking). Use darker shades to show the swirls and fill in using Yvonne's galaxy as your colour guide. Hook different colours or shades next to each other so the contrast emphasises the shapes. Yvonne used white fabric dots to give a starry effect against darker colour - these can be inserted later.

5. To finish off the edges of your hanging, first turn the side and bottom seams under, twice, and hem stitch them. To make a hanging sleeve, you can use carpet tape, or similar, a centimetre (½in) narrower than the finished width of your piece. Turn the ends of the tape under and stitch them so they will not get caught on the hanging rod. Now sew the tape to the top seam of the hanging, about a centimetre (½in) from the edge of the hooking, leaving the ends open to insert a rod (b). Hem the top seam to the back, like the others.

> ### TIP
> Yvonne mostly uses 0.6cm (¼in) wide strips but she always cuts and hooks a trial strip before cutting any more fabric. The loops must be wide enough to stay in, but not so wide that they are hard to pull through the backing.

> ### TIP
> You could chalk round some plates and a tray if you want a rough guide for your freehand sketch, then use marker pen to draw the spiral. You can modify the sketch using a different colour.

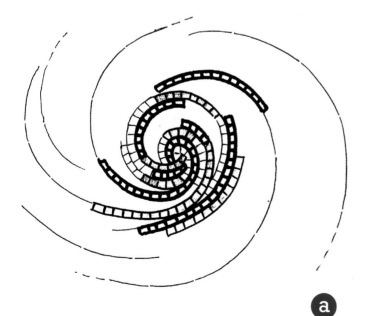

a

b

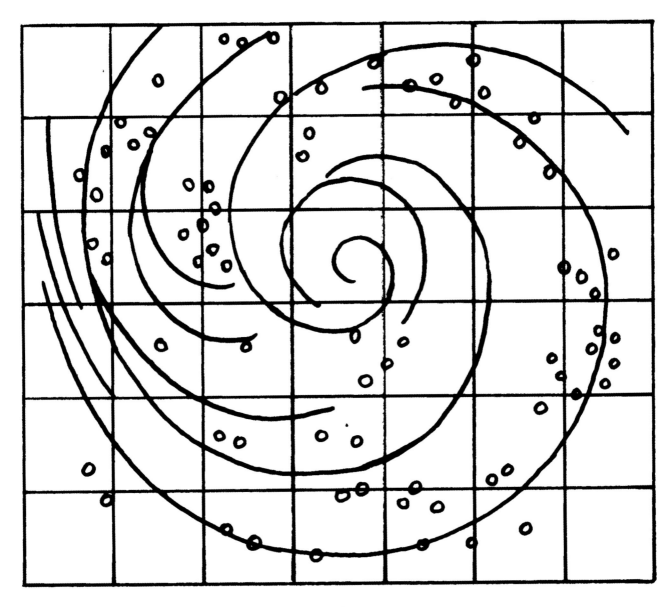

Galaxy hooked rug. Woollens 56 x 30cm (22 x 12in)
Coll ection of astrologer Steve Judd.
Both by the author

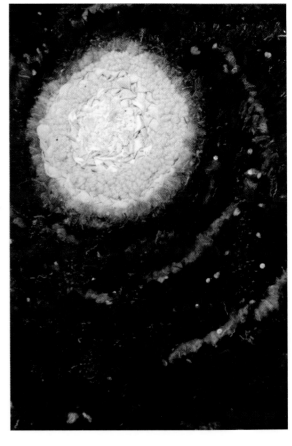

Detail of mixed technique galaxy, oval hanging.
Private collection.

Hooked brooch and pendant (inset) by Caroline Marriott, mixed fibres

HOOKED BROOCH AND PENDANT

Project 6 by Caroline Marriott

"This is a lovely way of using up all the little pieces left over from other projects. I have baskets full of snippets of thread and wool and small bits of beautiful fabrics that I cannot bear to throw away. Using the hookie method I turn them into little jewels."

YOU WILL NEED:

- 10cm x 10cm of hessian or linen scrim
- small amounts of a variety of wool and fabric
- card
- pencil
- marker pen

- scissors, sewing needle, pins, thread
- small piece of felt or other backing fabric
- PVA glue
- cord for pendant
- brooch back (available in craft shops)
- rug hook

INSTRUCTIONS:

1. Draw shape of BROOCH (choose size) onto thin cardboard and cut it out to make a template. Place the template onto the centre of your hessian or linen scrim and draw around it with the marker pen (a).

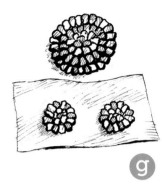

2. Take strips of fabric or lengths of wool and hook into the hessian (b) leaving the end of the strip on the back . If using thin wool, work 2 or 3 strands together. When changing colour cut off wool at back leaving 2-3cm tail.

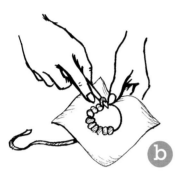

3. Use as many different fibres and fabrics as you like and work in blocks of colour or work from the outside towards the centre. Don't dot your colours all over the place as you will create a tangle of fibres on the back that you cannot hook through.

4. When you have hooked the entire shape (c) turn it over and trim any ends. With the wrong side of your work facing upwards cut around the shape leaving a 2 cm border. Snip into the border at 2cm intervals (d).

5. Turn the border under pulling the hessian tight, sew down (e). You may need to ease you brooch into shape at this point.

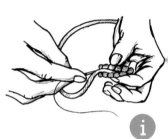

6. Use template to cut out a back for your brooch. You may need to cut the back a little larger than the template if you have used thick wool or fabric. Pin the back to the brooch and stab stitch them together (f).

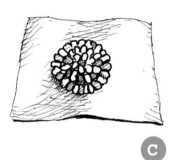

7. Finally attach a brooch back.

8. TO MAKE A PENDANT follow the instructions up to the point of sewing down the border on the brooch. (5 e)

9. Draw 2 circles with diameter about 1.5cm onto linen scrim. I draw around a little button. Hook into these as you did for the brooch (g). With wrong side facing, cut around the finished shapes leaving a border to turn in and sew down.

10. Measure out a length of cord to your requirements. Place one of the little circles face down and put a drop of PVA glue onto its centre. Place the 2 ends of your cord onto the drop of glue (h). Put a drop of glue on the second little circle and place over the two ends of the cord. Pick all of this up between thumb and finger and press together for a minute.

11. Stitch the 2 small circles together sewing through the cord as you go round (i).

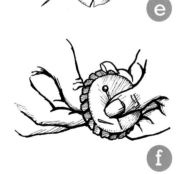

12. Put your unfinished brooch face down on the table and lay the mid point of your cord across the back. Stitch the cord in place. Finally, cut out a piece of backing fabric using your template and stitch into place (j).

Add stems for flowers

HOOKING WITH A SPEED SHUTTLE

I use a speed shuttle (shuttle hook) because it is quicker than working with a hand hook. The shuttle pushes a series of same-sized loops into the hessian from the back. The hessian must be stretched taut on a frame (see page 42). Like hand hooking, the aim is to form a dense loop pile so you can't see the hessian on the right side.

How to do it

I am right-handed and this is how I do it. Left-handers usually find it easy, but some prefer reversing the direction of travel.

1. Stretch the hessian on a large frame (see instructions on page 42), then draw your design on the back of the hessian. This means your design is a mirror image of what you will see on the front. Draw the outline of the rug and leave 10cms (4in) around the edge for the hem. Cut fabric strips about 1cm (½ to ⅜in) wide, along the weave, or from neck to waist if using jumpers.

2. With the frame leaning against a wall, work on the back (wrong side) of the hessian. Thread the strip through the small metal ring and up through the eye of the shuttle, leaving about 2cm (1in) dangling through the eye (a); let the strip hang down.

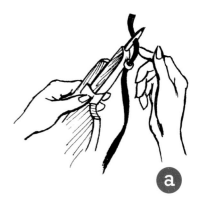

3. You can work the border first or an outline of a shape. Hold one side of the shuttle firmly in each hand. With the needle side in your right hand, push the needle between the hessian threads, all the way (b). Now push the left-hand side of the shuttle in and pull back the right side simultaneously (c), working along the line without 'walking' the shuttle. It makes its own steps, so you just push and pull, pointing it in the direction you want to travel. I work from bottom to top or left to right, working the outlines of shapes first, then filling in.

4. When you've used up the strip, thread another strip and continue where you left off. Poke the strip ends through to the front with something pointed like a bodger, to be trimmed level with the loops later. Work in lines next to each other so the front is covered in loops.

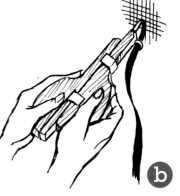

5. When you have hooked the whole rug area and trimmed strip ends level with the loops on the right side, cut the thread you used to stitch the hessian to the frame webbing and use one of the techniques in the section on finishing.

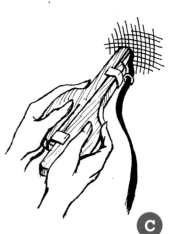

Tips on hooking:

- If it's awkward getting at part of the design, you can lift and turn your frame through 90 or 180 degrees, so you just work from the bottom to top or from the left to right (as I do).

- When I started using a shuttle I kept turning the frame round every ten minutes to trim the ends and see how it looked on the right side. Now I can work large areas before I look at the front.

- If the shuttle is stiff to work, your strips could be too thick – it should move smoothly and rhythmically, without difficulty. Try cutting your strips a fraction narrower.

- Take care not to push the point against a hessian thread - it should go between the threads. If you break a thread, sew on a small hessian patch which extends beyond the break, at least 5cm (2in), then work through the two layers.

- If hessian is visible on the right side between the loops, it probably means that you have 'walked' the shuttle rather than letting it move at its own pace. You can pull out the faulty strip and work it again, going more slowly and pushing and pulling the shuttle carefully so the loops are closer together.

- If you find a small detail is not clear on the right side, you could unpick it and hand hook it later from the front.

Hooking backgrounds

If you are not sure how far your materials will go, you can contour hook the background. That is done when you have worked an object or shape first, then you hook round it, line by line, working outwards, which is a way of blending different shades together. It also emphasizes the item you are surrounding. Early American rugs had backgrounds worked in meandering lines sometimes with little shapes, like hearts, embedded in them. If you are filling an area in a single colour you can hook it in parallel lines – if you are filling in a circle, you work in ever-decreasing circles.

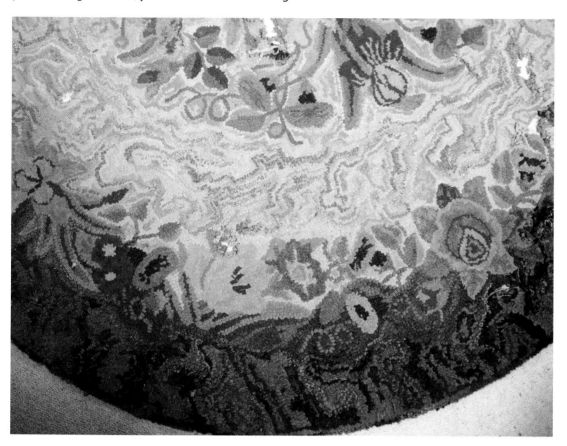

Vintage hooked rug from Louisiana – probably hand hooked on a commercial printed hessian. Note how the background was hooked. Mixed fibres

Hooked leaf rug by author. Woollens with contour hooked background using strips of blanket and hand-spun yarn.

Blending colours

To make a blended transition from one colour to another you can work in one colour, then introduce a row of a second colour, then a few rows of your first colour, then another of the second fabric, gradually spacing out the first colour until you are working exclusively in the second. This technique is useful if you want to break up a dense block of one colour, or if you don't have enough of one fabric to cover an area.

Detail of hooked hanging with blended background

Circular rug 1600cm in diameter (63in) made from recycled jumpers for a Scorpio client.

I made this rug with a speed shuttle around 1990. You can see how the zodiac was drawn as a mirror image, to be worked from the back. (I drew it the other way round first, and had to re-draw it on the other side when I realized my mistake!) I used some 15th century astrological figures and a Hereford bull (I live in Herefordshire), but when an archeologist asked me to make a similar one for her, I used a bison image from a cave painting to represent Taurus.

*Celtic knot hooked rug by the author.
Woollens, 60 x 80cm (appx. 24 x 32in).
Private collection*

CELTIC KNOT HOOKED RUG

Project 7 by Jenni Stuart-Anderson

"I hooked the rug in the photograph with a speed shuttle but you could use a hand hook, if you wish. It's a design which could be worked from the front with a hand hook or from the back with a shuttle. I cut machine knitted jumpers into strips because I like the way they hook but I also like to mix in hand spun yarn, hooked two strands together, for added textural interest."

YOU WILL NEED:
- large sheet of paper and pencil to enlarge template, unless you enlarge straight onto the hessian
- long ruler (straight-edge)
- marker pens in different colours
- 10oz common hessian, big enough for the design plus at least 10cm (4in) border to attach to frame and hem later

- a selection of machine knitted sweaters/yarns
- speed shuttle
- large frame with webbing attached to 2 sides (see page 41)
- scissors
- rotary cutter, ruler, board (optional)

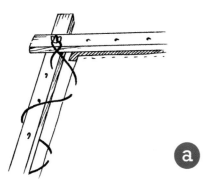

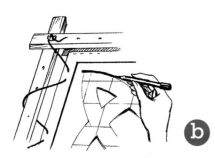

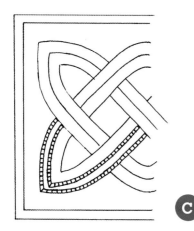

INSTRUCTIONS:

1. Sew the hessian on the frame (see page 41) leaving an aperture inside, big enough to accommodate your rug plus the border. Make sure you leave at least 7.5cms (3in) around the edges to turn under later. Stretch the hessian sideways by threading string through it (I use a bodger) and round the frame verticals (a), so you can tighten it later if it sags (due to ambient humidity). Tie the ends round the bolts.

2. Draw a rectangle on the hessian, defining the outside edges of your rug - you can rest a long straight edge against the frame as a guide for the horizontal lines.

3. Enlarge the diagram on next page, using grid system on page 30, to a size which will fit inside your drawn rectangle (b). You can either draw this on a large piece of paper, then onto the hessian (cut round the paper shape and use it as a template), or draw diagram straight onto the hessian, with the frame flat on table or floor.

4. Follow the instructions for cutting fabrics and for hooking with a speed shuttle or hand hooking. Start by outlining one knot in your first colour (c), then change colour and follow the other knot outline. Fill in the shapes. You could work the outside border next (d), or do it first. Work the background in lines following the outside edge of the knot (e), so you can blend varying shades as you use up one jumper and start another. All strip ends should be poked or hooked to the front and trimmed level with the loops.

5. When you have covered the entire rug surface with loops, cut the stitches which hold the hessian to the frame and follow one of the finishing techniques on page 96.

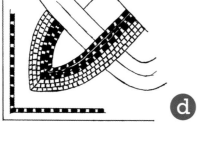

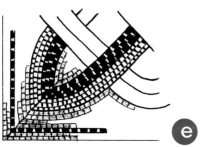

*Mixed technique rug by the author.
Mixed fabrics, size same as project 7.
(It was difficult to hide the plait ends
without making the rug lumpy)*

DIAGRAM FOR
CELTIC KNOT RUG

MORE RUGS/HANGINGS HOOKED BY JENNI WITH A SPEED SHUTTLE USING RECYCLED WOOLLENS

'Scorpio' 84cm (33in) diameter

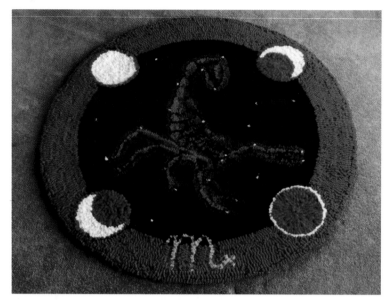

'Miss Penny's cats' 65 x 33cm (25½ x 13in)

'Baluchistan' 100 x 50cm (39 x 19½in)

'Best friend' 75 x 50cm (29½ x 20in)

PLAITING/
BRAIDING

In the 1930s and 40s people in the UK plaited laddered silk or lisle stockings to make mats (although, during the war, when they couldn't get stockings, they drew a line up the back of their legs and pretended they were wearing them!) In the Maritime Provinces of Canada they used to hook rugs using dyed silk stockings, and the practice of braiding strips of fabric to make floor rugs was common there and in North America, where they also used to make multi-strand braided borders for hooked rugs. In the 19th century the Swiss straw industry was flourishing and exporting plaited straw hats all over Europe. The settlers in North America who produced braided rugs would have typically worn plaited straw hats and bonnets.

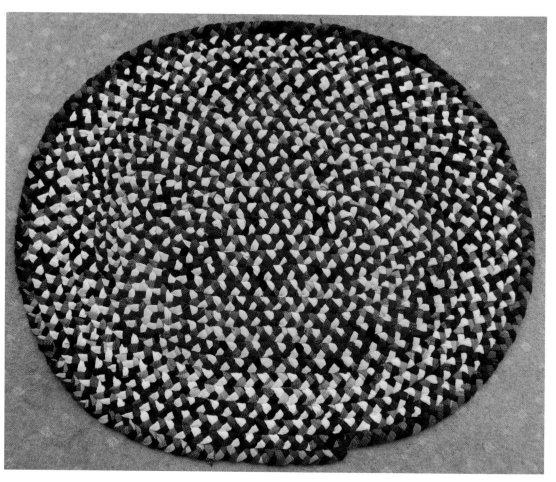

Braided rug from Nova Scotia. Cottons, 82 x 66cm (32 x 26in) Collection of Eileen Scholes

For plaited rag rugs I combine fabrics which are similar, such as all cottons, so they will wash evenly, although I do sometimes use different weight fabrics, like needlecord or velvet, alongside thinner cottons. To get an even, straight plait using different weight fabrics, it is necessary to make a short test plait or two, varying the width of the strips (for thinner fabric cut strip wider than for thicker fabrics) until you get a plait which sits straight. Or you can select similar weight fabrics and cut all the strips the same width. Try making test plaits using different width strips, to find which looks best for your chosen fabrics. Strips narrower than 5cms (2in) will make a very thin rug and it will be hard to conceal any raw edges. Test plaits can be as short as 30cms (12in) – save them for future reference as to strip widths.

I don't sew the strips into tubes (the traditional American way), I just turn the raw edges to the back, as I plait. Any frayed edges at the back are concealed when I back the rug with fabric and stitch it round the edge and across the plaits, to consolidate them. If you want a reversible rug you need to stitch the fabric into tubes first and there are plenty of American books showing how and including various devices you can buy (like Braid-Aids) which hold strips as you plait. I already find this technique rather slow – I guess I want quick results – so the table mat projects are simple, without special gadgets. Plaiting is, however, the best rag rug technique for showing off the surface of a fabric, and it has its own unique charm.

Detail of plaited rug made by the author from skirts, two table cloths, cotton ticking and a tee shirt. 80cms diameter (about 32in)

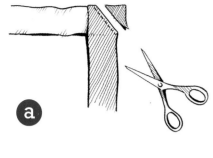

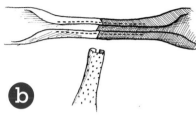

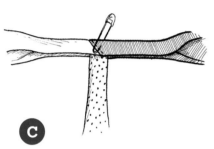

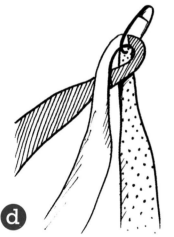

PLAITING/BRAIDING:
How to do it

1. Make a test plait (or two) to decide on the strip width which looks right for your chosen fabrics.

2. Cut or rip the fabrics into strips along the weave. If your strips are short (eg from a shirt), join them with diagonal seams (a). If they are cut from something long, such as a sheet, roll up one end of each strip and secure it with a pin, leaving a metre (yard) to work with as longer strips get tangled as you plait. Then you unroll another bit and re-pin as you go.

3. Start with 3 strips. For a spiral, join 2 strips(a) and folding the edges to the middle, lengthwise, place the top of third strip in the centre (b), (raw edges folded to back) which makes a neat centre for your spiral. For a rectangular rug, omit (a) and (b) and just pin 3 strip ends together.

4. Secure the strips at the top with a safety pin (c) and hook pin over something secure, or tie it to a chair back. Plait the strips by bringing the right-hand strip over the middle strip, so it becomes the new middle strip. Then bring the left-hand strip over the middle strip (d), and repeat (e, f, g).

5. To make a rectangular rug, lay some plaits side by side. To make a spiral or an oval wind one plait round. Join by lacing through adjacent plaits with strong thread in a bodkin (blunt needle), passed behind single strips of the plaits on adjacent sides so the thread's like a 'ladder' (h). Pull the thread gently to bring the plaits together. Lace from the back so the thread doesn't show on the front, keeping the stitching fairly loose so it doesn't pull and deform the finished piece (pointy hat anyone?)

6. For circular or oval rugs, you can either plait and lace together the central part, then join additional strips as they run out, plaiting and joining, as you go. Or, you can make a really long plait and then lace it into shape. The first way gives you control over when the colours change. The second, produces a more random effect.

Plaited cottons make good bath mats, as hessian backed rugs smell musty if they get damp. You can machine wash them too (I put mine in a pillow slip first). I had to retire this plaited cotton bath mat after 10 years, as I felt like a change!

Plaited sandwich cushions with foam 'cheese' by Jenni Stuart-Anderson. Mixed fibres, 33 x 23cm (13 x 9in)

Tips for plaited projects:

- Wider strips make fatter plaits which grow faster, but they need more lacing/stitching as the extra weight can pull them apart.

- If the laced plaits have some gaps between them, you could add some invisible stitching with needle and thread, from the front.

I zig-zagged this plait into a spiral using a sewing machine, then appliquéd the leaves on it. Cottons, 58.5cm diameter [23in]

TWO PLAITED (BRAIDED) TABLE MATS
Project 8 by Jenni Stuart-Anderson

SPIRAL TABLE MAT

*You can make this table mat any size you like or make a matching set.
The one in the photograph is 23cm (9in) across and was made from old clothes in 3 different colours (a skirt and 2 blouses).
If you make a thicker, bigger spiral it could be a seat mat or a rug. Why not start with a table mat and see if you'd like to make a plaited rug later?*

YOU WILL NEED:
- assorted cotton fabrics for plaits and backing
- blunt needle (bodkin or lacing needle)
- strong thread for lacing
- a sewing needle and thread to match your fabric
- pins
- scissors
- safety pin
- sewing machine (optional) for joining strips

TIP
200cm (79in) long strips will make a 20cm (8in) diameter spiral mat.

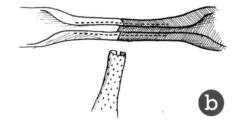
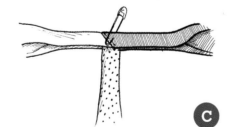

INSTRUCTIONS:

1. Choose fabrics of similar weight and cut or rip the fabric along the weave into strips 7.5cms (3in) wide. Join strips (a) so you get three strips 2.65m (105in) long, to make a spiral 23cm (9in) diameter.

2. Roll and pin the strips leaving about a metre (1yd) unrolled, to plait.

3. Join 2 of the strips together (as a) and fold the edges to the middle and stitch about 15cm (6in) (b).

4. Fold the edges of the third strip to the back, place it on (b) then fold so edges meet (c). Push large safety pin through centre, hook it over something steady and holding the three strips towards you, start plaiting (the point where safety pin passes will form centre of spiral).

5. Turning the raw edges of the strips to the back, as you go, plait the 3 strips (d) following instructions for plaiting/braiding, until plait is about a metre (1yd) long.

6. Working on a table, pass a needle and thread through the pointed end of the plait and start winding it into a spiral, securing it by stitching right through the plait, until it stops trying to un-curl, when the spiral is about 10cm (4in) in diameter. The stitches should not show on the front. Knot the thin thread to thicker thread and change to a bodkin.

7. Working from the back, start lacing the plaits using the threaded bodkin which you pass behind adjacent strips (e). Lacing should not show on the front. Work with the spiral flat on the table and keep it soft and pliable. If you pull too tightly, it will curl up.

8. Continue plaiting and lacing to within 15cms(6in) of the strip ends, then cut them so they taper to half their width (f). Plait and lace to the end. Tuck the tapered plait end to the back and stitch neatly.

9. Place the mat on the backing fabric and cut round it leaving a border (or seam allowance) of 2.5cm (1in). Turn the mat upside down, pin the backing on it, turning the border under round the edge. Pin and sew the backing neatly to the mat, around the edge.

VARIATIONS:

- For a spiral larger than a table mat, you will need to extend the strips by adding on more strips: plait, lace, add on, plait, lace etc. Join strips so the seams aren't next to each other which would make the plait lumpy.
- For a larger item, like a rug, the backing will need to be held in place by back-stitching across the plaits at right angles as well as stitching it around the edge.
- You could make a number of small spirals and arrange them in a circle on a table, then stitch them together where they touch. Then you could stitch a long plait, or two, around the edge to hold them together.

RECTANGULAR TABLE MAT

YOU WILL NEED:
- same as for spiral table mat

INSTRUCTIONS:

1. Choose fabrics of similar weight and cut or rip the fabric along the weave into strips 7.5cms (3in) wide. Join strips, as for Table Mat 1, so you get three strips 2.65m (105in)

2. Safety pin ends of 3 long strips of fabric together. Roll up the other ends leaving about a metre (1yd) unrolled, to plait.

3. Hook pin over something steady and turning the raw edges of the strips to the back, plait them, following instructions for plaiting/ braiding.

4. Make 9 plaits, about 30cms (12in) long, securing ends with pins. Arrange plaits side by side on a table so the colours please you. Lace two plaits together, working from the back using strong thread and bodkin passed behind adjacent strips. Lacing should be visible only on the back. Work with the plaits flat on a table; don't pull the thread too tightly. Lace plaits together until they form a rectangle. You can lay them on a sheet of writing paper, as a guide (a). Trim ends straight.

5. Binding ends of mat: cut two strips of fabric 7.5cms (3in) wide and a little longer than the mat width, and pin, then stitch it across the plait ends, turning the two edges over at sides (b).

6. Cut a piece of fabric for the backing, a bit larger than the table mat, fold side edges under, towards mat and stitch together neatly.

7. Fold the end binding strips under the mat, covering the ends of the backing. Tuck raw edges under, pin, and stitch down neatly.

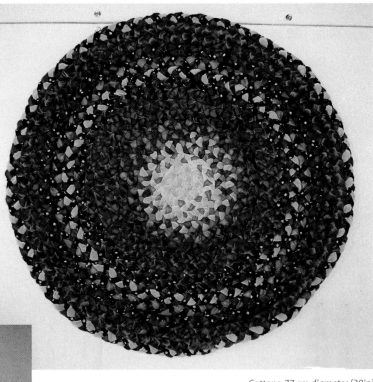

Plaited rugs by the author.

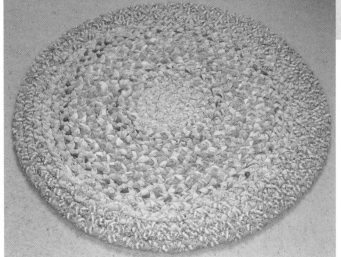

Cottons, 77 cm diameter [30in]

Cottons. 81cm (32in) diameter

"Fire" rug for storyteller Ben Haggarty to take into schools for the children to sit round. Mixed fibres/ techniques, by the author

MIXING TECHNIQUES

By mixing techniques you can create really interesting textural contrasts and exciting combinations. I have made plaits to frame hooked wall hangings and sometimes progged a border on a hooked piece.

If you want to mix techniques on a floor rug you need to think about any difference in density which could feel uneven, underfoot. Here is a progged rug with a separate hooked ammonite laid on it first, then the progging done, round the ammonite, through two layers of hessian, so joining them. To raise the hooking to the same level/thickness as the progged surround, I sewed some quilter's wadding under it, between the ammonite and the rug beneath.

Progged rug with hooked ammonite by the author. Woollens, 92 x 31cm (12 x 36in) Private collection

Back view

I have made quite a few mixed technique spirals, which I start with a plait sewn onto the hessian backing to define the spiral. Then I fill in with progging, line by line, then hooking – it's like painting with fabrics. Before starting I select some fabrics which look good together and then build up the piece, sometimes adding or taking out fabrics depending on how they look, worked next to each other.

Mixed technique hanging by the author Mixed fibres, 75cm dia. (30in). Private collection

Raggy brooches by the author

Site specific hanging by the author
Mixed media, 2metres high (78in)

"I am making all things new" by the author. Mixed technique commemorative
hanging in an Essex church. 130 x 50cm (51 x 20in)

On the workshops I facilitate around the UK, I can often tell who has done a City & Guilds textiles course because they usually choose to make a sampler to try out different techniques. You could do that too, and keep it for future reference. Or you could use a hessian bag as the backing for your sampler, like the ones on the customized bag pages.

Mixed technique hanging by the author from a London
Transport poster. Mixed fibres, 75 x 45cm (29½ x 18in)
Private collection.

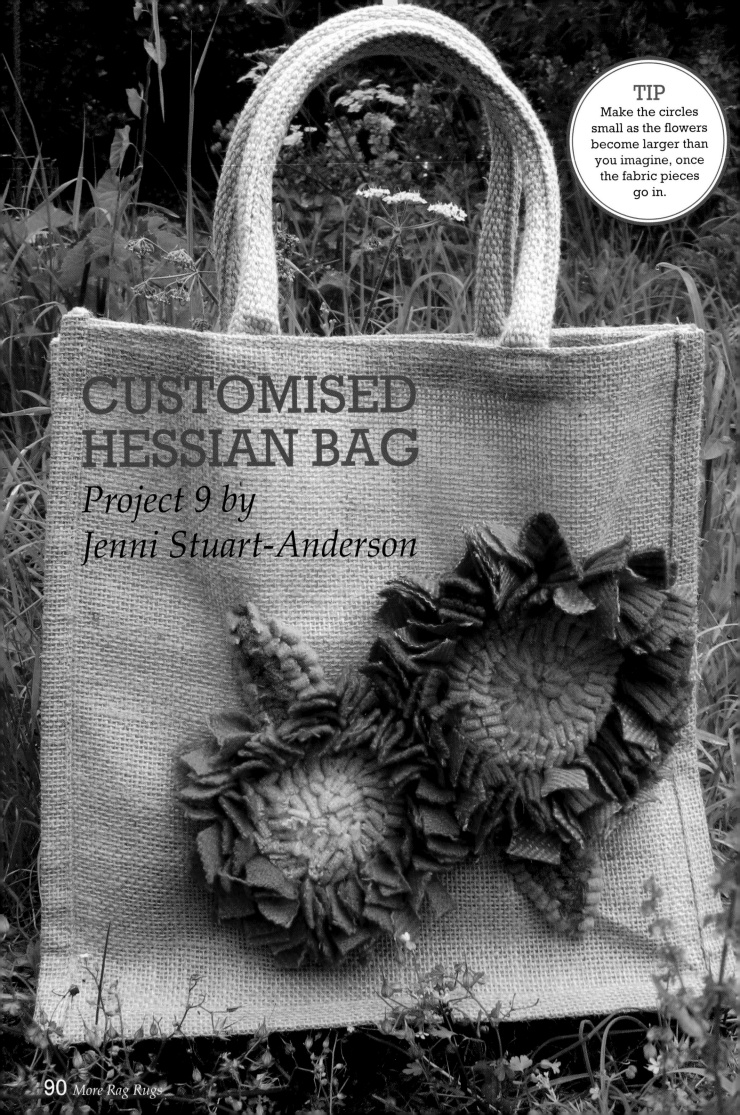

CUSTOMISED HESSIAN BAG

Project 9 by
Jenni Stuart-Anderson

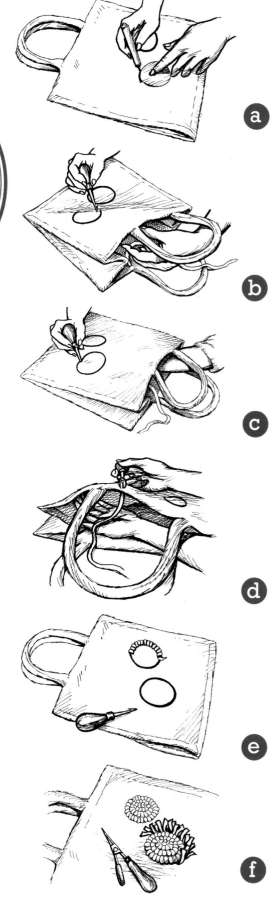

A customised hessian bag is a really useful sampler where you can try out different techniques. If you use a hessian bag which has a stiffener on the inside surface, you can hand hook it without a frame. The first one I decorated– people kept asking me where I bought it as walked around with it over my shoulder! They make great presents.

YOU WILL NEED:

- a hessian bag, preferably stiffened
- a selection of yarns and fabrics
- a rug hook
- a bodger
- scissors
- marker pen
- lid to draw round

TIP
Start with a small design. You can add more but you can't unpick without it showing. So start with one or two flowers, then add a little at a time, like painting with rag, unless you want to cover the whole bag.

INSTRUCTIONS:

1. Draw one or two circles round something like a jam jar lid to make the flower centres, leaving space between circles for the bulk of the petals (a). You could start with just one flower and add more when you have worked it and can see how it looks.

2. Cut a strip of fabric, to test for the right width for hooking. Try 0.635cm (¼in) wide for thick fabric and a centimeter (⅜in), for thin. If it breaks when hooked, cut slightly wider. Or hook one to three strands of wool/yarn, depending on thickness.

3. Taking the hook in your writing hand, above your drawing, hold the strip of fabric or yarn in your other hand inside the bag, with the bag resting on the table in front of you (b). Poke the hook into the bag, between the threads(c) but only about a centimetre (½in) as you have to be careful not to break any threads. Offer the end of the strip to the hook, inside, and pull the strip end to the top, holding the bag on the table with the back of the hand inside it (d), which is easier than it sounds.

4. Follow the instructions for hooking on page 65, working round the circle. Because you can't work from all sides of the bag, hook the circle from right to left, first one half, (e) then the other. Fill in the circle with loops working in the same way, leaving 2 threads of hessian between loops. Pull the loops up about a centimetre (½in) high.

5. Cut the material for the petals into pieces about 7 x 1.5cm (2¾ x ¾in), wider if material is thin. Using the bodger follow the progging instructions on page 53 working round the circle you hooked (f). Depending on how it looks, you can prog one or two circles of petals.

6. Fill in the other flower(s) and if you feel your design would be enhanced by some leaves or stems, you can add them, hooking or progging.

More bags customised by the author

Mixed technique hanging by Lorenzo Gavarini. Mixed fibres
83 x 74cm (32½ x 29in)

Mixed technique made by members of Age Concern, North
Herefordshire, with the author for Home Front Recall, part of
Veterans Reunited Lottery programme to commemorate the
60th anniversary of the end of WW2.

PEGLOOM WOVEN RUG
Project 10 by June Emmerson

The pegloom was developed in the mid 1980s and derives from ancient weaving sticks used to make braid. There is a list of components in this section, next to a picture of a pegloom, which could enable you to make your own.
June made the rug below from a mixture of oddment knitting yarns, various cut-up clothes and sheeps' wool, in a range of predominantly greens and browns.

Rug woven by June on a pegloom.
Mixed fibres, 112 x 58 cm (44 x 23in)

YOU WILL NEED:

- pegloom with 30 pegs
- threader (optional)
- warp thread (dishcloth/craft cotton or any strong, thick cotton that doesn't break when pulled)
- knitting yarns: a mixture of plain, textured and mohair
- fabrics of similar, medium, weight eg cotton tee shirts, trousers, skirts
- small quantity of carded dark brown sheeps' wool (optional)
- sharp scissors

TIP
If you are new to pegloom weaving, weave a small sampler first, to give you confidence in the techniques. Your sampler could become a cushion cover, seat mat, or wall hanging.

Weaving rag strip

INSTRUCTIONS:

1. Remove thick seams and cut clothing into strips about 5cm (2in) wide and as long as possible. Cut tee shirts in spirals to get long strips, starting at the bottom. Cut trousers in spirals up the legs, or lengthways in strips.

   Knitting yarns: wind together several strands to produce a super-chunky yarn which speeds up the weaving process, using some textured yarns or mohair to add interest.

   Washed and carded sheeps' wool would add good texture and colour.

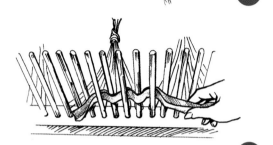

2. **Warp up pegloom**. Cut your warp thread into 30 lengths, each one 260cm (102in) long. Sitting with the pegloom on a table in front of you, thread each warp through the hole on a peg, using a pegloom or needle threader. Bring the 2 ends together and put the peg into a peg hole. Leave the warp threads dangling, until they are all threaded, then tie them in bunches of 7 or 8 with a couple of loose knots to prevent tangling (a).

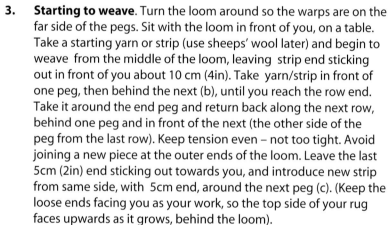

3. **Starting to weave**. Turn the loom around so the warps are on the far side of the pegs. Sit with the loom in front of you, on a table. Take a starting yarn or strip (use sheeps' wool later) and begin to weave from the middle of the loom, leaving strip end sticking out in front of you about 10 cm (4in). Take yarn/strip in front of one peg, then behind the next (b), until you reach the row end. Take it around the end peg and return back along the next row, behind one peg and in front of the next (the other side of the peg from the last row). Keep tension even – not too tight. Avoid joining a new piece at the outer ends of the loom. Leave the last 5cm (2in) end sticking out towards you, and introduce new strip from same side, with 5cm end, around the next peg (c). (Keep the loose ends facing you as your work, so the top side of your rug faces upwards as it grows, behind the loom).

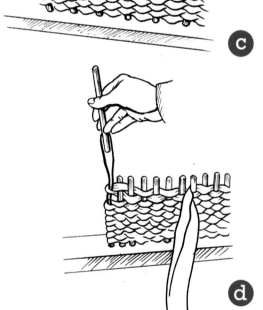

4. When weaving reaches 2cm (¾in) from the top of the pegs, transfer it off the pegs onto the warp threads. Right-handers, start at left end (loom in front of you, warps behind it) and left-handers, at right end.

   Take the first peg out of its hole, taking care not to let any other pegs jump out at the same time. Pull the peg up vertically and draw it out right through your weaving (d). (Twist as you pull it, if it's stiff to get out). Once clear of the weaving, replace peg back in its hole. Repeat, lifting each peg along the row and replace (e) being careful not to let 2 adjacent warp threads get looped over each other. Continue weaving and move your work off the pegs each time it nears the top.

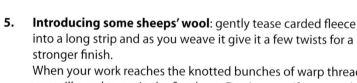

5. **Introducing some sheeps' wool**: gently tease carded fleece into a long strip and as you weave it give it a few twists for a stronger finish.

   When your work reaches the knotted bunches of warp threads you will need to untie the first knot. Don't worry if your work looks very loose at this stage, it will all tighten up later.

6. When weaving reaches no less than 24cm (9½in) from the end of the warp threads, take it off the loom. Make sure you have woven enough rows to bunch up tight, for a strong, thick rug.

   Finishing off is best done on a large, rectangular table. Remove all pegs, carefully, and lay them flat on the table. Untie slipknots at the opposite end, and pull the pegs gently through your weaving a little way, to make the warp ends equal at each end. Then, cut the warps from the pegs. Tie them, in pairs, into a half-knot (f) at both ends to keep the weaving from wandering. Using the right angles of the table, take time to tease your rug into shape. Hold outer edges and tug to straighten the rows. Bunch up your weaving, or spread it out more in places, to get an even thickness. You can use your fingers like claws to pull the weaving about. You may need to retie some warp half- knots to get a good straight top and bottom edge. Once you are happy with the rug shape, finish tying the warp ends. Leaving half-knot in place, tie a simple overhand knot over the top of it (g). Trim the ends, leaving at least 5cm (2in). The loose ends of your weaving can be tucked in behind and woven over one or two rows with your fingers.

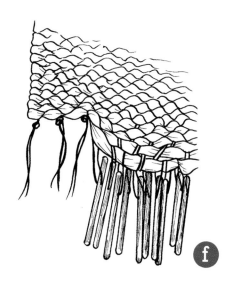

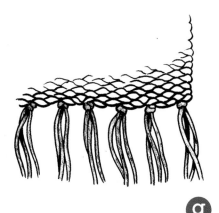

A Pegloom with threader
For most purposes, ideal timber sizes are:
9mm (⅜in) dowel rod cut to 13cm (5in) lengths, 4.5 x 7cm (2 x 3in) timber board drilled at 2cm (¾in) centres, to depth of 2.5cm (1in) to hold pegs x length to suit. A long board will hold more pegs, to weave a wider rug.

TIP
The pegloom is a voracious eater of whatever textiles you can feed it with. Thicken bold coloured/textured knitting yarns by weaving them together with plain yarns: ideally, they need to be thicker than Aran weight.

Rugs woven by June from mixed fibres.

Ammonite hooked by author using hand spun yarn and Wensleydale rare breed fleece

Vintage instructions

FINISHING & CLEANING RAG RUGS

FINISHING RAG RUGS

I have been told that most prodded or progged rag rugs were not backed (lined) as dirt could get trapped between two layers of a floor rug and wear it out from the inside. Having said that, there's always someone whose granny used to back her rugs. One woman said her gran used a sack, prodded one layer, then inserted dry newspapers every night to soak up the damp as people wiped their feet on it.

Unbacked rugs are more flexible and drape more, so a wall hanging will benefit from a backing to stiffen it. The backs of progged rugs look a bit like mosaic. I have been told they used to have rag rugs upside down in the week, and the right way up on Sundays. I usually back hooked, plaited and mixed technique rugs but not progged ones. It's fine to hem a hooked rug too.

Here are some finishing methods:

READY-MADE HEMS

> *We only had them right side up when the doctor called.*
> Durham

Before you start your rug, you could turn the edges of the hessian over once to the top and stitch them by hand (see Mizzy Mazzy project 1), then you prod, prog or hook through two layers round the edges and more at the corners. This technique gives a very neat finish but it is slower working through more than one layer.

My teacher used to start a rug by progging a border of four rows, then turn under and hem stitch the edges. This way, the hessian didn't fray whilst she worked the central part of the rug during winter evenings.

HEMMING

Fold the unworked edges under twice at the back of the worked area, pin then slipstitch, making sure to catch the backing fabric and not progged or hooked pieces.

For rectangular rugs the corners of the hessian can have the point cut off then be folded (a and b), the edges folded twice, pinned and stitched (c), making sure to stitch through the hessian, not progged pieces.

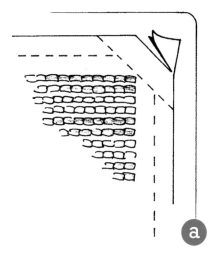

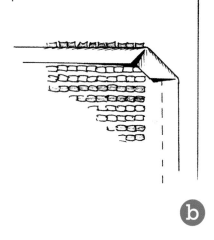

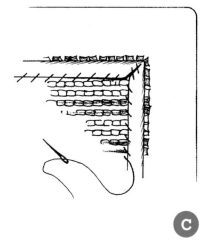

In Northumberland they fold over the edges, put piping cord, then oversew with wool or strong carpet wool. Then they put tape all round the back of the rug.

If you want to make a rug which is an irregular shape, think first how you will finish the edges. Curved borders need to be snipped so the hem will sit flat, then when you fold the border back you will need to oversew where you snipped, so the hessian doesn't fall apart. Quite tricky and not recommended for beginners.

Wool and mohair fabric rug, progged by author , Approx. 70 x 54cm (27½in x 21in)

BINDING

Cut off any surplus hessian, leaving a 3cm (1¼in) border around worked area (d). Pin cotton carpet tape (or similar tape) on the right side of the hessian and backstitch a line close to the worked area using strong thread (e). Make sure you join the ends of the tape on a straight side, not a corner of the rug. Ease the tape round any corners or points.

Turn tape to the back, pin, and hemstitch it to the rug with strong thread (f). This will produce a neat line of binding all around the rug which shows only from the back.

Some prefer this method – it is useful if you have inadvertently worked too close to the hessian edge.

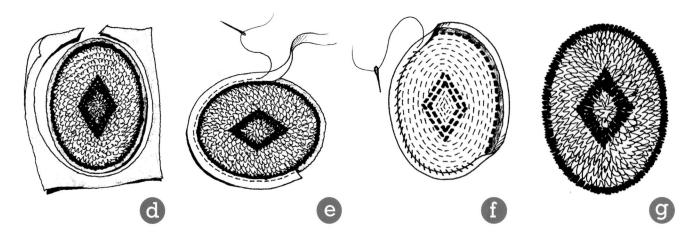

FABRIC BACKING

I back seat mats with fabric turned under and stitched around the edge. They are cushion sized and usually have layers of wadding in the middle.

TIP
You could cut up and recycle a synthetic duvet to pad seat mats.

GLUED HESSIAN BACKING

This is suitable for mixed technique pieces when the back looks a bit messy, or for hooked rugs, if they are going to be wall hung.

Cut away any surplus hessian, leaving a border of 3cm (1¼in) around worked area. Cut another piece of hessian slightly larger than the worked area to use for the backing. Spread a very thin layer of latex carpet adhesive over the back of the worked area doing a strip about 30cm (12in) wide at a time. Place the backing on the glued area and smooth it down with your hands. There should not be enough glue to come through the backing.

Repeat this process until the whole of the back has hessian stuck over it, then trim it so it covers only the worked area, leaving the hessian border.

Fold the border back, mitring corners, and glue it down lightly over the edges of the backing (h). Glue carpet tape, or similar, to cover the raw edge of the border, mitring the corners (i).

TIP
Put some adhesive in a saucer and use a knife to spread it thinly – just enough to stick it but not enough to soak through the backing. Always use such adhesive in a well ventilated place, wear an apron, maybe gloves, and follow manufacturer's instructions.

WORKING ON A SACK

> *Flour used to come in a white sack and we would wash them and cut them up to make napkins for a new baby.*

If you can get a jute hessian sack, you may find that when you undo the string holding the sides together and open it out, it has two selvedges. You could turn the two shorter ends about 5cm (2in) to the top and work through the two layers. Then you could work right up to the long selvedges without needing to hem them.

CLEANING RAG RUGS

In the UK, before vaccum cleaners, rag rugs were hung outside over a washing line and beaten with a wicker carpet beater to get the dust out.

In countries where snow is common in winter, people used to place their rugs upside down on the snow and walk on them, so the powdery snow acted as a dry cleaner.

I sometimes vacuum rugs when I am making them and when they are finished, if the materials shed a lot (they stop fraying, eventually). Some people tell me they just throw their rag rugs in a washing machine but I hand wash them in the bath, leave them to drain, then put them outside to dry. I lay them flat over a ladder or netting so the air circulates as they are too heavy to hang on a washing line, especially when damp.

When I have used a commercial machine to shampoo fitted carpets, I have also done rag rugs. The cleaner spreads, then vacuums away proprietary carpet cleaner diluted with water.

I do machine wash rugs progged on white, open weave rug canvas, but pin them inside a pillow case first. It is important that the edges have been stitched well so the action of the washing machine doesn't fray them. This works well for plaited cotton mats too, which is why they make good bath mats.

> *On the farmhouse floors the peg mats would get covered in grease and get a shine to them: all the goo was polished (you didn't wash them).*
> Huddersfield

GALLERY

Here are profiles of the makers who have contributed to this book plus some other rug makers and pictures of their work and some projects sent to me by people who have been on my workshops. Some are accomplished makers, others were beginners who became hooked on it!

'Homage to Rothko' Progged rag rug
Woollens, 61 x 53cm (24 x 21in)

JENNI STUART-ANDERSON

"Working as a freelance designer whilst teaching at Hammersmith College of Art & Building, I decided to move to the countryside aiming at a lower impact lifestyle, which now includes recycling locally sourced textiles.

So many people asked me how to make rag rugs that I started offering workshops, locally at first, then across the UK. Some students send pictures of rugs started on my workshops and I feel privileged to have helped ignite their creative enthusiasm.

Sometimes I make rugs inspired by traditional designs but I also enjoy pushing out the boundaries of a heritage craft whilst helping to keep it alive by spreading the word.

Experimenting on a recycling theme with 3D work, my Kitchen Escape series included wings made from 50 pairs of rubber and work gloves and a flying machine made from a laundry drying rack with reclaimed push chair wheels: did it fly? (don't ask).

European development funding helped me to start weaving which opened my eyes to the remarkable world of spinning, weaving and rare breed sheep. I love fabrics, especially tweed (if only there were more hours in a day!)"
www.jenni.ragrugs.freeuk.com

Progged wreath made for Doris Tunley's funeral

'One more pair and I'm off!' mixed media hanging, 1.5meters wide

Mixed technique hanging by Jenni. Woolens 112 x 112cm (40 x 40in)

A selection of Eileen's work including progged Christmas tree

Natasha helping Eileen

EILEEN SCHOLES

"As a nurse by profession, I first started making rugs working with elderly patients suffering from Alzeimer's, as a way of encouraging social interaction. It did! And I have been making for the last twenty years, giving workshops and enjoying the fun of jumble sales in order to obtain raw materials.

I work to commission, teach and demonstrate the craft around Cumbria, including at Farfield Mill, the leading venue for textile arts in the North West."
em@scholeskl.co.uk

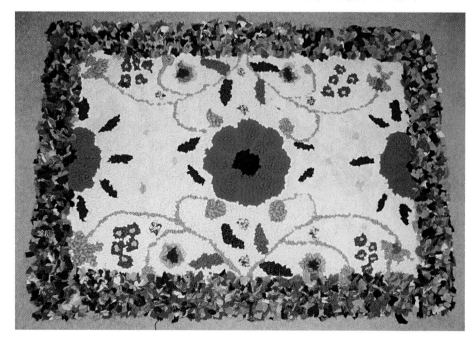

Eileen's first hooked and progged rag rug

A hooked hanging from a drawing by Ruth Scholes

'Waves'

'Dunes' Progged hanging

YVONNE AUTIE

"My first experience of rag rugs was in 1994, when my husband retired from the RAF. I heard Ann Davies lecture at the Harrow Embroiderers Guild and I was sold on the idea of hooking! Soon afterwards I saw Jenni demonstrating rug making and signed up to do a day course with her. Jenni introduced me to the bodger and started me on the bathmat that is still in daily use. She also convinced me of the benefits of the speed shuttle.

Yvonne with hooked hanging of Arfa

Our loft is fully insulated with huge, transparent sacks of fabric waiting to be turned into rugs. I have learnt a lot from numerous rug makers & now teach others the joys of rug making. Animals and the local landscape plus my garden inspire me. I acquire fabrics from any charity shop that does not support animal testing.

Time is divided between designing and making jewellery and textiles. Somehow my husband manages to fit into a house

'Clarence' Miixed technique hanging

where there are projects in progress in almost every room and a Spanish Galgo stretching long legs on the sofa. All dogs love the proddy mats I made that are in front of the wood-burning stove."
yvonne_autie@dsl.pipex. com

'Pink Fizz' mixed technique bag with plastic tube handle

Tea cosy with progged plastic bags

Hooked brooches and bangles. Mixed materials

CAROLINE MARRIOTT

"I started my textile career crocheting little stripey jumpers for fellow students at University. I went on to do a teacher training course and for many years combined working in school with developing my own work.

I enjoy playing with colour and was drawn to rag rugging because, as with all my work, I can use a wide variety of materials and a very large palette."

www.carolinemarriott.com
marriott.caroline@googlemail.com

Mixed materials, pegloomed rugs

Sheep's fleece, pegloomed rugs

JUNE EMMERSON

"I first started serious weaving on a pegloom when I moved to Shropshire in 2005. I found a local smallholder with Herdwick sheep who was having to burn her fleeces because the Wool Marketing board wouldn't take them. A few years and many rugs later, I started to mix materials and spin up my own extra chunky yarns from recycled knitting and industrial yarns, a highly creative process in colour and texture, using up to 25 different yarns spun together. I began to add fabrics sourced largely from local charity shops' unsaleable rag.

For the past few years I have enjoyed running workshops and teaching pegloom weaving to old and young and people with special needs. Making peg[l]ooms and the chunky yarn became a necessity. Following a visit to the Outer Hebrides in 2010, I am now using Harris Tweed selvedge waste ribbon sent to me by some of the weavers. This was previously thrown away. I am currently part of a craft textiles co-operative which promotes the use of local and sustainably sourced materials. I relish this opportunity to share my passion with others."
www.woollythinking.org.uk

Rag pegloomed rug

Cotton rugs progged by Lorenzo who drew the illustrations for this book

'Tropical'

'Tree of Life', detail

LORENZO GAVARINI

"Rag rugging can be adopted as a hands-in way of painting: obtained from old garments, the tridimensional fraying brush-strokes are held between one's fingers, the canvas' docile weave accommodating their crowding progress into any design... or at least, that's how I first got into it, as a means of creating tactile images with ever surprising textural effects.

Once Jenni had introduced me to feverish Jumble Sales and sleepy Charity Shops, I acquired a fashion taste for the ready-to-tear and also started filching from her many store-bags.

Learning from Jenni the traditional techniques, rekindled my neglected passion for painting which, alongside illustration and lace design I used to practice back in Italy, many years ago.

Eventually, painting regained priority over the more sporadic work with hooks, pegs and rags but I continue to be delighted by the wealth of invention, wit and aesthetic talent shown by the many practitioners of this popular craft with its endearing treasure of memories and anecdotes."
lorenzo.gavarini@yahoo.co.uk

DEBBIE SINISKA

Debbie is a textile artist, felt and bead jewellery maker who offers regular workshops in Kent, where she lives, East Sussex and other places. She is Jenni's daughter's auntie and has written books on bead jewellery and on rag rug making (see further reading).

"This tactile and practical art has captivated me over the past 20 years and by choosing colours and textures that attract you in the first place artistic self-expression will have already begun to work for you. Working with simple hand tools and scraps of ready to hand reclaimed textiles is fun and comes with a sense of achievement."
www.debbiesiniska.co.uk

'Fantasy Leaf' hooked rug

Hooked Green Man hanging

'Flotsam' hooked wall pieces

Mixed technique brooches

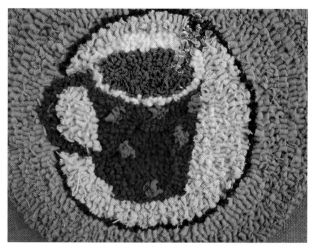

Hooked tea cup seat mat

MARGARET PARKINSON

Margaret's daughter in law told Jenni about the wonderful hookie rugs made by Margaret since the 1970s. Margaret lives north of Carlisle.

"The elderly farmer next door gave me a set of mat frames and I acquired several hooks from my aunt. I entered the picture of Beaumont in a show but the judges thought the sheep and cows should have had more legs. As a member of the local bowling club I made sketches of bowlers and the clubhouse with the Solway in the background.

I was asked to demonstrate rag rug making at a WI event and set up the dresser design. I would love to own a dresser but do not have space for it so this is the next best thing.

I always work on hessian stretched on a frame and draw a rough plan using a black permanent marker. As it takes several weeks to complete I find I want to add or take away as my ideas develop. I experimented with all kinds of fabrics and found that patterned material could give interesting effects. Anything goes."

Rugs hooked by Margaret Parkinson

Hooked rug and progged rug made by Helen Parkinson taught by Margaret

" *You had your range which you polished on a Sunday morning with Zebrite and your rag rug in front of it. I lived in a back-to-back in Aston in Birmingham so I can tell you all about poverty.* "

" *My gran used to make rag rugs in the Lake District. She had three daughters and a son so every fourth year we'd get a new rug.* "

Collie dog hooked by Hazel Wilson whose husband is a shepherd in Northumberland

WORKSHOPS

Rag Rug Workshop

The rhythm of the rags
And the rhythm of the words
Are like the surging of the sea.

Hands fold, cut, grip, pull, swim
Through swirling, many-coloured
depths.
Torn edges are white surf
Rippling over hessian sand.

And the tide of voices
Rising and falling
Follows the rhythm
Of the cutting and the hooking
As we recycle and braid together

Rachel David
July 17-20, 2006
Marlborugh

Jenni's drop in taster workshop at Ludlow Green Fair 2010

ELIZABETH TURNER

In 2005 Liz first invited Jenni to do a workshop at the Thomas Shop, which she runs with her husband Derek in mid Wales where they have restored a village shop from 1805 and set up the Wool Emporium, celebrating wool and textile art and design across Wales. They offer regular craft courses and accommodation and there is a cafe/tea room.
www.thomas-shop.com

Rug progged by Liz on a rainy holiday on Lleyn Peninsula, Wales from materials sourced from Red Cross shop in Pwllheli

"My Granny Nichols was fantastic knitter and crotchetier. Granny Knevitt produced beautiful and sought after embroidery that went round the world-especially for church vestments…..I was to inherit her leather suitcase full of embroidery silks and work in progress. My mother was very ingenious and productive making things from scraps around the home. I had no knowledge of rag rugs until I emigrated to Canada aged 21 and came across the wonderful plaited rugs made by the indigenous Indian population and sold along the roadside but made with love and enthusiasm from the limited resources they had available."

'The tiger who came to tea' was made over 18 months for Liz's daughter Ellie

SUE RATCLIFFE

Sue and Jenni became friends after they met on a workshop. Sue has been to subsequent workshops and owns several rugs made by Jenni. Sue sells her rugs from her narrow boat and at craft markets around Gloucestershire; she also passes on rag rug making techniques which are traditionally associated with narrow boats.
www.raggytaggyrugs.co.uk

Proggies for sale

Sue on the narrow boat which she shares with Callum

EIRLYS PENN "PROGGING ROCKS"

(from **www.scrapiana.com** blog by Eirlys Penn)

> " *The little circular mat was made by my grandmother for a doll's house, probably mid-twentieth century, if not earlier. My plaited attempt is supposed to be a kind of homage to that.* "

"Proggy – it's rough beast. I decided to make it very irregular throwing all kinds of odds and ends into it, leaving the seams on the denim and not measuring the pieces at all. Scraps include dad's old dressing gown, gingham left over from wedding bunting. I quite like the out-in-the-woods lumberjack feel of the end result. It's what I call a hap rug after hap quilts which were not really designed, just worked for utility, however they happened to develop."

> " *Pretty much as soon as I got home, the cat found the proggy. Jenni assures me this is quite normal feline behaviour.* "

Hap rug…seat mat…hap mat started by Eirlys at Jenni's workshop at the Museum in the Park during the Stroud International Textile Festival in 2011.

PAT LEMON

Rugs hooked without a frame by Pat Lemon who came to a workshop at the Blue Ginger Gallery in Worcestershire in 2011.

Rug progged by Pat Lemon's friend Liz Greatwich, started on a subsequent workshop at Blue-Ginger Gallery

John Dyer, who attended a taster workshop at the Festival of Quilts, threading his frame. Doris's sheep rug made by John from a project in Jenni's book Rag Rug Makingand a rug which he hooked..

A tea cosy made by Jen Gibson after a plaited rug workshop.

Festive Wreath made by Chris Walker

Two rugs hooked by Lindsey Malin with her speed shuttle

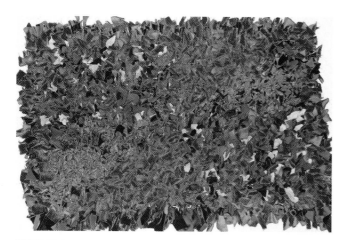

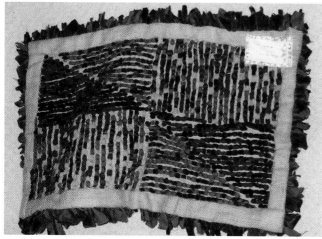

Rug made by Sue Glover on a Country House rug weekend in Shropshire

Joan Aket started this progged rug at a workshop and it now sits in front of the fire at Pakenham Water Mill, Suffolk where her husband is a volunteer. The mill has wheat delivered in sacks and the rug is made on half a wheat sack.

Colleen Baker's progged cotton rug

" *Oh rag rugs – I really want to have a go but I couldn't take home stuff for ANOTHER craft: my husband would leave! Hmmm…. (thinks)…but then I could keep my craft stuff in his half of the wardrobe.* "
A visitor to Jenni's stand at the Knitting and Stitching Show 2011

Anon

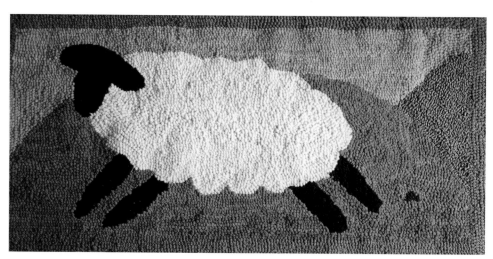

Ann Middeton's first hand hooked rug

PLACES OF INTEREST

Acton Scott Historic Working Farm
Acton Scott Hall, Acton Scott,
near Church Stretton, Shropshire SY6 6QQ
tel. 01694 781307
www.actonscott.com
Keeps alive 19th century farming practices and period skills

The American Museum in Britain
Claverton Manor, Bath BA2 7BD
tel. 01225 460503
www.americanmuseuminbritain.org
American folk and decorative arts

Beamish Museum
Beamish, County Durham DH9 0RG
tel. 0191 370 4000
www.beamish.org.uk
*Recreates the Georgian, Victorian and Edwardian periods
in the North*

Berrington Hall
near Leominster, Herefordshire HR6 0DW
tel. 01568 615721
www.nationaltrust.org.uk/berringtonhall
Neo classical mansion with Capability Brown gardens

Birmingham Back to Backs
50-54 Inge Street/55-63 Hurst Street
Birmingham B5 4TE
tel. 0121 666 7671
www.nationaltrust.org.uk/backtobacks
Restored 19th century courtyard of working people's houses

Black Country Living Museum
Tipton Road, Dudley DY1 4SQ
tel. 0121 557 9643
www.bclm.co.uk
Over 50 authentic shops, houses, workshops

Farfield Mill
Garsdale Road
Sedbergh, Cumbria LA10 5LW
tel. 015396 21958
www.farfieldmill.org
Restored19th century mill with exhibitions and events

**Forge Mill Needle Museum & Bordesley Abbey
Visitor Centre**
Needle Mill Lane
Riverside, Redditch, B98 8HY
tel. 01527 62509
www.forgemill.org.uk

Nantwich Museum
Pillory Street
Nantwich, Cheshire CW5 5BQ
tel. 01270 627104
www.nantwichmuseum.org

Museum in the Park
Stratford Park, Stratford Road
Stroud, Gloucestershire GL5 4AF
Tel. 01453 763394
www.museuminthepark.org.uk
*17th century wool merchant's mansion with exhibitions of
arts and applied arts*

St.Fagans National History Museum
Cardiff CF5 6XB
tel. 029 2057 3500
www.museumwales.ac.uk
*Open air museum in grounds of St.Fagans Castle.
Over 50 original buildings from historical periods*

The Thomas Shop
Maesyfed, Penybont
Llandrindod Wells, Powys LD1 5UA
tel. 01597 851951
www.thomas-shop.com
*Restored shop museum dating back to 1805 also sells
Welsh crafts*

FURTHER READING

American Hooked and Sewn Rugs by Joel and Kate Kopp, University of New Mexico Press, June 1995

From Rags to Riches by Rosemary Allan, The Beamish Collections 2007

Handcrafted Rugs by Sandra Hardy, Guild of Master Craftsmen Publications, 2001

Rag Rugs by Ann Davies, New Holland, 1996

Rag Rugs by JuJu Vail, Quintet, Apple Press 1997

Rag Rug Inspirations by Juliet Bawden, Cassell 1996

Rag Rug Making by Jenni Stuart-Anderson, Traplet Publications Ltd. 2003, 2007, 2010

Rag Rugs of England and America by Emma Tennant, The Decorative Arts Library, Walker Books, 1992

Rag Rugs Old Into New by Debbie Siniska , DHGM Ball 2010

Rag Work by Lizzie Reakes, Lorenz Books, 1996

Rare Hooked Rugs by William Winthrop Kent, the Pond-Eckberg Company, 1941

Rugs from the American Museum in Britain by Sheila Betterson, The American Museum in Britain 1981

Rugs from Rags by John Hinchcliffe and Angela Jeffs, Orbis Publishing, 1977

SUPPLIERS

Jenni Stuart-Anderson and Lorenzo Gavarini
The Birches
Middleton-on-the-Hill
Herefordshire HR6 0HN
tel. 01568 750229
www.jenni.ragrugs.freeuk.com
Commissions, tools/equipment, books, courses. Illustrations.

Brown and Cook Ltd.
77 Allcock Street, Birmingham B9 4DY
www.brownandcook.co.uk
Hessian etc.

Creative Grids (UK) Ltd.
Unit 1J, Peckleton Lane Business Park
Peckleton Lane, Peckleton
Leicester LE9 7RN
tel. 01455 828667
www.creativegrids.com
Rotary cutters, mats etc.

Rigby Cloth Stripping Machines
Route 302, PO Box 158,
Bridgton, Maine 04009, USA
tel.207 647 5679
Fabric strip cutters

Makings Handicrafts
7b Roydon Road
Launceston, Cornwall PL15 8DN
tel. 01566 779136
www.makings.co.uk
Rug tools

CRAFT AWAY WITH OUR EXCITING RANGE OF BOOKAZINES, BOOKS AND DVDS

RAG RUG MAKING

BY JENNI STUART-ANDERSON

Let Jenni Stuart-Anderson lead you on a journey through a fascinating world of rag rugs that will have you well and truly hooked!

The book looks at: the history of rag rug making and effective ways to make rag rugs, with clear, step by step diagrams. It includes information on tools and equipment, hints on planning, designing and marking out rug patterns, projects to try yourself, anecdotes and reminiscences about the craft, together with dozens of contemporary rugs made by Jenni and other modern rug artists.

Ref: RAG2

RIGHT FROM THE START

The Basics of Patchwork and Quilting

BY BARBARA CHAINEY & CHRIS FRANSES

If you're new to Patchwork and Quilting and keen to know more, this book will guide you in easy-to-follow steps through all the basics, so that you can be sure that you really do get it right, right from the start. With an abundance of tips and easy to follow step-by-step instructions, they guide you through all the stages of making patchwork by hand or machine.

Ref: RFS

APPLIQUÉ - A CUSHION A WEEK

BY GRETA FITCHETT

Exploring different techniques of appliqué, with projects for beginners and experienced crafters, including simple hand-stitching, machining and bonded appliqué.

Includes templates and a materials list.

Ref: APP

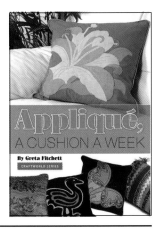

STAINED GLASS PATCHWORK FOR CHRISTMAS

BY GAIL LAWTHER

Create spectacular stained glass patchwork designs for the festive season with this fantastic book by award winning quilter, Gail Lawther.

Ref: SGP

STAINED GLASS PATCHWORK 1 (DVD) - BASIC

BY GAIL LAWTHER (APPROX 60 MINS)

Take the mystery out of stained glass patchwork with this fantastic DVD by Gail Lawther, detailing easy ways of using this very quick and dramatic technique.

Ref: DV705

STAINED GLASS PATCHWORK 2 (DVD) - ADVANCED

BY GAIL LAWTHER (APPROX 60 MINS)

Discover many ways to vary, embellish and develop the basics of the stained glass patchwork technique to create your own unique quilts.

Ref: DV706

INSPIRATIONAL STRIPPY QUILTS

Beautifully photographed in colour, Inspirational Strippy Quilts is a bookazine featuring a short history and patterns from a 1930s quilted strippy; it then looks at newly made strippies pieced in traditional designs and moves on to contemporary piecing and appliqué designs.

Ref: PQSP11

INSPIRATIONAL PROJECTS

This colourful bookazine from the publishers of British and Patchwork Quilting magazine presents 12 fantastic inspirational patchwork, quilting and appliqué projects. Whether you're looking for inspiration to make decorative textiles to enhance home décor, or seeking great gift ideas, you're sure to find something that suits.

Ref: PQSP10

INDIAN INSPIRATIONS

BY GISELA THWAITES

Simple Indian style embroidery stitches and techniques and how to use them, including: fabrics, threads and beads, and working with shisha (mirrors).

Ref: IND

TWO BY TWO PATTERN BOOKLET

BY LESLEY BRANKIN

Create a heirloom quilt that will be loved by successive generations. This pattern booklet contains comprehensive instructions and full size master templates. (intermediate/advanced level).

Ref: TBT

DOWN ON THE FARM

BY LESLEY BRANKIN

Foundation piecing pattern booklet for this lap-sized quilt, inspired by "Old MacDonald had a Farm", with instructions, colour plates of animal blocks and full-size master foundation templates (intermediate/advanced level).

Ref: DOF

QUILTS UNCOVERED 1 AND 2 DVD BOXSET

BY JENNIFER BARLOW

In this two-disc set, Jenny shows how to take pattern design elements from traditional and contemporary quilts to create a beautiful and unique quilting pattern for your next project, whatever its size and shape.

Ref: DV717
Also Available on Blu-Ray
Ref: DV717HD

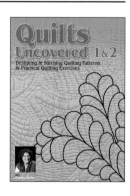

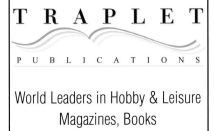